GROOVY, MAN

First Warbler Press Edition 2023

ISBN 978-1-959891-80-2 (paperback)
ISBN 978-1-959891-81-9 (e-book)

warblerpress.com

GROOVY, MAN

Staying Alive Through
the Psychedelic Sixties,
Greenpeace, and Matrimony

DAVID TUSSMAN

In Florence the hero David
rises in marble above all men.
There is no sign now
Of that small boy who dared
But only that pride, that force, that gloried brow,
That destiny,
The godhead bared.

There is another David,
Small, divided between child and man
Who dreams his fate
And holds his world concealed
While on the rim of this arena he waits,
That moment
The seed of deity revealed.

—Lorrie Tussman

CONTENTS

THE TRIAL

In 1973 when 1 was a miserable second year law student at
Hastings College of the Law in San Francisco's Tenderloin
District 1 would wander over to the Federal Building to
look in on the LSD trial of the century. There, 1 listened spellbound to the testimony of Billy Hitchcock, heir to the Gulf
Oil fortune, former patron of the psychedelic movement,
owner of the Millbrook estate where Timothy Leary once
lived. But Hitchcock, facing twenty years in jail for his role in
the manufacture of Orange Sunshine, the LSD that defined
the era of the late Sixties, had turned government informant
and was testifying against his two former accomplices, Nick
Sand and Tim Scully, the chemists who had built the labs and
produced the millions of doses of the highly prized Orange
Sunshine. For me, this was a window into a magical world
in which 1 had played a small part, but now 1 slipped into the
courtroom unnoticed and unknown.

Described elsewhere as tall handsome and charming, in
court Hitchcock appeared to me as slightly pudgy and bland,
not projecting a lot of charisma as he testified in a monotone
voice about the details of those heady days: arrangements
with Sand and Scully to set up labs, arranging distribution
through the Brotherhood of Eternal Love, vainly attempting
to manage the unraveling of their psychedelic empire as various law enforcement agencies slowly closed in for the kill.

A defense lawyer, attempting to undermine his testimony, queried Mr. Hitchcock, "Have you used LSD?"

"Yes," he replied.

"Heroin?"

"Yes."

"Amphetamines?"

"Yes."

"Cocaine?"

"Yes."

"And were you high on any of these substances during your meetings with Mr. Sand and Mr. Scully?"

"No," he deadpanned.

Sand and Scully, by contrast, filled me with awe. Nick Sand, short and tightly wound, could have passed as a preppy college student. He was a true believer, a psychedelic warrior for life who would never yield an inch in his beliefs. He seemed to view his current circumstances merely as a speed bump in his mission to turn on the world. I had first spotted Scully standing outside the courtroom chatting with his lawyer, Michael Kennedy. Thin, pale and ethereal looking, dressed in an ill-fitting three-piece suit, he seemed fragile and out of place in this sterile courtroom environment. Far more nuanced than Sand, by the time of his indictment he had given up his brief career in the world of psychedelics and moved on to other things, his original faith shaken by what he saw as the failed promise of LSD to transform the people who took it or society in general. A beautiful woman accompanied them who I first thought was Scully's girlfriend but later learned was Kennedy's wife Eleanora. Kennedy, who looked the epitome of an East Coast Irish Blue Blood lawyer, was developing a reputation taking on notorious clients and would soon move to New York where he would leverage his notoriety to ingratiate himself as a society lawyer best known for representing Ivana Trump in her divorce from Donald. He was smooth and composed but nothing I saw convinced me he merited any particular acclaim as a litigator. In fact, I quickly concluded that in this case he was selling his clients down the river.

Given the evidence it would have been unconvincing for the defendants to deny that they were the masterminds behind the manufacture of Orange Sunshine. Instead, Kennedy concocted a preposterous defense to the effect that Orange Sunshine was a perfectly legal substance known as ALD52, not the prohibited LSD25. There was only one problem— actually, two problems. First, the making of ALD52 required a step in which you first synthesized LSD25. To circumvent this problem, they claimed that Scully had devised an alternate synthesis that skipped that step. The second problem was the fatal one: once synthesized ALD52 tended to decompose back into LSD25, and that is indeed what the seized substances tested as. Any fool could have seen this defense was going nowhere, especially in front of the impassive Judge Stanley Weigel, who doubtless had nothing but contempt for these privileged kids who had thrown it all away in their misguided effort to turn on the world.

To establish their defense Scully, the master chemist, had to take the stand. "Have you ever taken an IQ test?" Kennedy inquired.

"Yes," he replied.

"And what was the result?"

"I was told that my intelligence was such that they were unable to quantify it."

Scully indeed projected an aura of genius. As a young math and physics student he had built a linear accelerator as his science project, worked for the Lawrence Livermore Lab as a summer intern, and started a computer consulting company, but his life took a detour after trying acid and deciding the world would benefit if everyone could have that experience. He hooked up with Owsley, the legendary underground chemist, worked with him as sound engineer for the Grateful Dead and learned from him the synthesis of LSD, ultimately leading to his collaboration with Billy Hitchcock, who financed the operation. Scully built a lab in Windsor, a small town north of San Francisco, where millions of doses of Orange Sunshine would be produced. His testimony attempted to paint Hitchcock as the real mastermind who was escaping responsibility by turning state's evidence. He had put both Sand and Scully on monthly retainers of a thousand dollars each, certainly not a princely sum, even in those days. Billy had an airplane which he operated under the umbrella of a whimsically titled company called Trans Love Airways, after the line in a Jefferson Airplane song. Supposedly he had promised the plane to Scully, but the gift never materialized. Perhaps Scully was making LSD only because he was hoping to get that airplane?

Sand never testified, which was probably a good decision. But he was humanized by the regular presence of his obviously devoted and attractive mother, and by the testimony of an ex-lover, a beautiful former Wellesley student he had met at Millbrook. She testified to Nick's interest in communal living. Did this explain his visits to the Brotherhood of Eternal Love, the loose organization of Orange County hippies, sometimes called the "Hippie Mafia," which smuggled huge amounts of hashish and became the main distributors of Orange Sunshine?

"And why did you break up with Mr. Sand?" his attorney asked.

"I fell in love with someone else," she replied, casting a wistful glance at Nick as she left the courtroom.

Sure enough, when the gavel came down it was fifteen years for Sand, twenty for Scully. Scully would be a model citizen, report to prison to serve his time, and be released after only a couple years helped by his work designing computer interfaces to assist the disabled. He went on to study psychology and biofeedback and had a successful career as a software engineer. Sand, on the other hand, continued his outlaw ways, skipping to Canada while out on appeal bond, not to be caught for twenty years when he was found running a huge LSD manufacturing operation in Vancouver. Sent back to the United States by the Canadian authorities, he wound up serving a drastically shortened version of his original sentence before his release. Until his death in 2017 he enjoyed his role as an elder of the psychedelic movement, but he no longer (we assume) played any part in its manufacture or distribution.

I was neither a genius like Scully nor a true believer like Sand, yet somehow I was able to find my own niche in the psychedelic underground of the 1960s.

A NORMAL BIRTH

I was normal when I was born. My mother reports I had the loudest cry of all the newborns in the maternity ward. Perhaps that cry was one of horror, realizing where I was and what I knew lay in store, the long slog of a joyless, tedious and unfulfilling life. It should not have been that way. Mine was a relatively privileged birth, the first wave of the baby boomers, destined to grow up on the golden shores of California, the son of a university professor and his beautiful, intriguing wife, blessed with intelligence, good genes and health. What could go wrong?

My father and mother met when my mother was a freshman at Cal living in International House in 1942. From an unremarkable blue-collar family in San Diego, she developed intellectual aspirations and had come to Berkeley to study and learn, to grapple with ideas, to gain understanding and wisdom and hopefully to do something to help heal the world of its pain and misery. But professors she visited to discuss ideas had only the idea of chasing her around their desks. Her beauty was legendary, but she rejected all suitors until she met my father, finally a man who respected her and took her ideas seriously. For the first time she found herself falling in love. A former Berkeley graduate student himself, my father was now in the army and had been sent to International House for an intensive six-month course in Mandarin before assignment to China as an intelligence officer. On the train to the east coast on his way to China he made a fateful decision, sending for her to meet him in Pennsylvania where they were married. Then he headed off to Kunming where he spent the next two years gathering intelligence on Japanese activity in China and presenting daily reports to the American and Chinese generals.

Toward the end he was given a dangerous assignment: he and another officer were to fly to the coast to help prepare for the anticipated American invasion of mainland China. The first day, their flight was canceled due to inclement weather. As they were about to leave the following day they received word the mission was cancelled. The atomic bomb had been dropped on Hiroshima and there would be no need for an invasion.

By now a major, my father eagerly looked forward to a return to Berkeley, but probably not without some apprehension. For the entire two years he had written almost daily letters to my mother. Frequently, but not quite as often, she would reply, until one day her letters stopped abruptly. Frantic efforts were made to get in touch until finally my mother confessed, she had allowed herself to be seduced by a young professor from Spain who introduced her to flamenco and charmed her with his passionate Latin soul, so much the opposite of my father. Arriving back in Los Angeles he was greeted by my mother, who had been staying with his parents. She noticed but didn't dare mention that in his two-year absence he had lost most of his hair. They decided to reacquaint themselves by going on a ski vacation to Truckee. There in a rustic cabin in the snow I was conceived, doubtless by accident or carelessness.

It turned out my mother was not exactly the nurturing,

maternal type. Her interest was in ideas, not the tedium
of running a household. The stress of marriage and moth-
erhood drove her to the verge of a nervous breakdown. My
father, somewhat conventional in his thinking, had hoped
to land a traditional faculty wife like the ones his colleagues
had married, someone who would dedicate herself to raising
a family and creating a beautiful home where he could host
lively dinner parties. "Gracious living" he called it, something
my mother refused to have any part of. Later she would write,
"He wanted a strange and complex wife—and then wanted
her to be satisfied with cooking elaborate meals, entertaining
and enjoying cocktail parties—and staying out of the intellectual world (except as a hostess) of which he was a part."

My mother holding me as an infant

She refused to consider owning a home; possessions, she
said, were an encumbrance on the spirit. He came to regard
my mother like a stray kitten, a rescue wife, whose extreme
sensitivity rendered her unable to survive in the world on her
own. Unable and unwilling to fulfill my father's expectations,
she was equally thwarted from pursuing her own dreams.

She wanted to get a PhD and do something significant in the world, but my father discouraged it thinking, perhaps correctly, that she was not cut out for the cutthroat competitive world of academia. And so my mother found herself trapped at home caring for a new baby, a life she had never wanted or imagined. There were no nannies, babysitters, daycare, or preschool to give her any relief. For the first five years of my life, we were together almost every moment. As for me, I had few playmates and little opportunity for socialization.

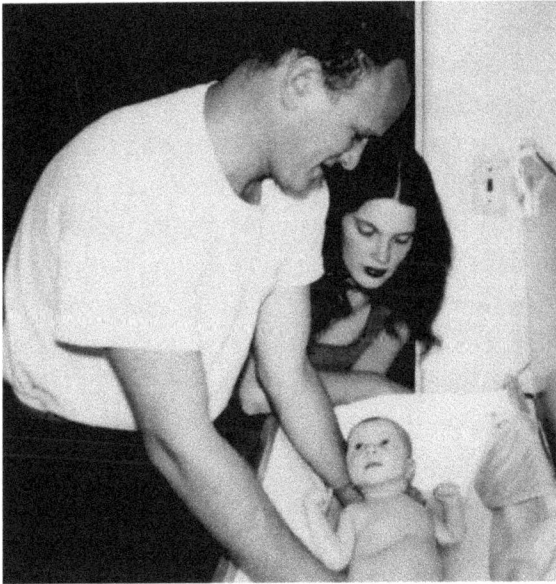

Joseph, Lorrie, and me

I must have sensed that my primitive needs and demands caused only upset and anxiety on my mother's part. Years later I would observe her preparing a chicken for dinner, fumbling awkwardly as she removed it from its package, holding it uncomfortably as far away from her as possible, exactly as I imagined she must have handled me as an infant. As for my father, his view of child rearing was *laissez faire*: leave them alone and they would turn out okay. But he insisted on keeping me on a strict schedule; I could cry as much as I wanted but would be ignored until it was time for my bottle.

Eventually I realized I was not going to get what I needed from the world and just gave up, retreating into myself and becoming as guarded and self-sufficient as possible. Never would I express love for my parents; we called each other by our first names. To my parents, ideas were all that mattered; I sensed that to them family seemed like an inconvenience, a bothersome obligation.

Forever doomed to be renters due to my mother's aversion to home ownership, when I was three we moved to a tiny cottage on Thornhill Drive in Montclair, a suburb of Oakland. The owners rented to us on the condition that we care for their cats, who quickly multiplied to a herd of over twenty with whom I had to compete for my mother's attention. I recall the day the Korean War started: June 25, 1950. Listening to the news on the radio, my mother said to my father, "I hope they don't take you!" Of course, they didn't, but I was left with the dread of knowing that the curse of being a male was having to go to war. The curse of a female was having babies. I wasn't sure which was worse.

Somehow my mother managed to continue work on her master's thesis in political science entitled *Insurrection and the Development of a Legitimate Opposition in Burma.* In those heady post World War II days, it was assumed that the newly freed Asian and African colonies would quickly develop into modern liberal democracies on the western model. One look at what Burma became reveals the naiveté of that optimism.

Several times a week my mother and I would walk up Mountain Boulevard to the Montclair Lucky store. On the way we passed an elementary school playground filled with happily frolicking children. I would look down in horror at that tangled mass of humanity with the awful knowledge that someday I would be thrust into that fearsome crowd to fend for myself. Didn't it appear they were merely having fun? No! It looked to me more like Hell, limbs flailing about, bodies colliding, bloodcurdling screams, senseless chaos. I knew I would be an alien in that world.

Lorrie as a student at Berkeley, 1942

Moving back to Berkeley from nearby Montclair, I started school at Hillside Elementary. The first day, waiting for my mother to take me, I became anxious, afraid we would be late. She was taking way too long in front of the mirror, doing something to her face, slapping her cheeks to improve her color. She was preparing for her moment of freedom, the first time she would be able to venture back onto the Berkeley campus on her own in five years.

My mother was always writing, and I wanted to write too. I composed stories in little spiral notebooks about my collection of stuffed animals, led by Teddy, a basic brown bear, who decided to run off to the forest to live with the animals to get away from his "grouchy" mother. But one day I grabbed Teddy, took him down to the garage and eviscerated him with a kitchen knife, discarding his remains behind an unused sandbox. This inexplicable act of violence was deeply disturbing. Why would I murder this innocent animal who was my totem, my alter-ego, my constant companion and best friend? I have no answer. But the scar from this senseless act lingers.

Sure enough, my horrific vision of the playground became a reality. During lunch recess, kids would jump on top of each other creating a huge squirming pile. I watched in horror, imagining what it would be like to be trapped at the bottom of that scrum of humanity, helplessly suffocating, panicking, struggling to get free. I would lurk about on the playground, trying to avoid engagement with anyone, and that must have attracted attention. I don't recall the specifics, but apparently other kids started taunting and chasing me around. It must have gone on for some time, until finally I got the courage to tell my mother, who dressed up and went to talk to my teacher. The taunting stopped, but I was left with another scar that would mark me for life. From that point forward my goal in school was to remain inconspicuous, to avoid interaction with anyone.

On the tennis courts after a mud bath at UC Berkeley, circa 1954

In the winter of 1955, we moved to Syracuse to begin what would become a seven-year stint on the East Coast. We left Berkeley because my father, by now an assistant professor of philosophy, was not granted tenure at UC. I missed Berkeley although I'm not sure why, since I wasn't really happy there. I became chronically depressed and at times wished my life to end, although in retrospect Syracuse sounds idyllic. There was snow—lots of it—and I loved the snow. We went skiing in winter, swam at Lake Skaneateles and spent summers at Chautauqua where my father taught summer school. The pizzas at The Villa with its jukeboxes at every table were delicious, as was the pastrami at Meltzer's Deli and the ice cream sodas that you could find everywhere. I even had a couple of friends, along with one tormentor not worthy of note. My tennis coach introduced me to a girl my age named Merilyn, and together we were the top players our age in Syracuse, traveling to junior tournaments until I got tired of losing and decided I hated tennis. Merilyn, on the other hand, always won.

Next door to us in our modest rental lived a traditional middle-class family with frilly curtains and a Chevy Bel Air in the driveway. I wished we were normal like them, but my mother wore toreador pants and played flamenco records.

Unlike in Berkeley where I had been just one of many bright students, in Syracuse I was identified as a "brain." I was also called "queer" on occasion, but in my innocence I thought that just meant "strange," and on that point I could not argue. I was left alone on the playground; it was an awkward Jewish kid named Roy who instead was relentlessly taunted and chased. I observed with sympathy, being confirmed in my belief that children were monsters. Or at least boys were.

I did well in school and was a model student, only raising concern on one occasion. The comic strip *Rex Morgan, M.D.* introduced a character who was a junkie, and I was intrigued. On my school papers I drew stick figures of a junkie with a hypodermic needle captioned, "I need a fix!" My teacher called in the principal, who called in my parents. "Where did you learn about drugs?" I was asked. "From a comic strip," I replied innocently. "A comic strip?" "Yes, Rex Morgan, M.D." My teacher came to my rescue: "Yes, I read that strip too."

Unhappy to be separated from the intellectual life of Berkeley, my mother developed horrible rashes and was clearly miserable. My implacable father didn't seem to mind where he was, although they still fought bitterly over his unfulfilled desire for gracious living. Feeling revulsion at everything American and the crassness of its culture, my mother desperately wanted to explore Europe, but my father had no interest in travel. So finally, when she felt I was old enough to be left with my father (age eleven) she departed on her own for six months touring Europe on a shoestring, staying in the cheapest pensions, falling in love with Spain, Portugal and Latin culture in general.

I graduated from Berkeley High School in 1964 and entered the University of California at Berkeley as a freshman. We had moved back to Berkeley the year before when my father was invited back as a tenured full professor. My academic record in high school was mixed, but I qualified for admission at UC thanks to my SAT test scores. During my last year at BHS I hardly spoke to anyone, achieving almost total invisibility. I had no friends and stumbled through the halls of school like a klutzy ghost. Teachers might have thought I was an enigma hiding deep and grandiose thoughts, but to me it seemed I was only hiding confusion and puerile inanity. If I had to express an opinion on a serious matter my brain would spin hopelessly out of control as I desperately sought to put tangled fragments of thoughts and words together, starting sentences not knowing how or where they would end. Upon graduation I had a joyous feeling of liberation, finally freed from the horrible prison of school. College, I hoped, would be a different experience.

The summer of 1964 was an idyllic time on the Berkeley campus, before the upheavals soon to come would forever change what was once called the Athens of the West. Sproul Plaza and the adjoining Telegraph Avenue were to be swept by waves of political protest and as the waves receded the new counterculture would take hold. But in the summer of

'64 Telegraph was still a quiet street lined with genteel book and record stores, Pauline Kael's Cinema Guild, a Jaguar dealership, and sophisticated home furnishing stores like Frasers and the Able 1 which offered all the accessories required for gracious living.

To get a head start on my college career I enrolled in an introductory physics class. I liked physics and got an A. When not in class I was entertained by a classic Berkeley character named Lenny Glaser who would install himself at the corner of Bancroft and Telegraph and give extemporaneous lectures designed to foment revolution. I was fascinated by his encyclopedic knowledge of everyone from Erasmus to Marx. He'd spent time in Moscow, which he felt was superior to Berkeley because the libraries were open twenty-four hours a day. He espoused a radical left-wing philosophy that I had once identified with. At the age of thirteen I had converted wholeheartedly to socialism, probably based on some favorable comment by my parents. I had a somewhat naive view of life under socialism, imagining it to be like a big summer camp where delicious meals would be served in communal cafeterias. No one would work too much because, in the common delusion held by leftists at the time, society was approaching an end to the age of scarcity and most mundane tasks would be automated, freeing people to live a life pursuing their fantasies, erotic and otherwise. Of course, it would first be necessary to be liberated from imperialist capitalism through violent revolution, but that seemed just around the corner. The brave idealism of socialism appealed to me. Fidel Castro was my hero—he had actually led such a revolution. I constructed a shrine to him in my bedroom. Flip a switch and my tape recorder would play Lawrence Ferlinghetti reciting his poem "One Thousand Fearful Words for Fidel Castro," whose endless speeches I would listen to, without comprehending, on Radio Havana using my short-wave radio.

Berkeley had the Young Socialist Alliance, the Socialist Workers Party, the Socialist Labor Party, the Communist Party and probably many others. I would furtively collect their publications from news racks around campus, hoping no one would see me. Something told me my radical beliefs needed to be hidden. I never actually met anyone from these organizations, but was puzzled by the fact that these groups seemed to loathe each other as much as they loathed capitalism. I wanted to be part of a movement that was untainted by the pettiness of internecine conflict, that shared my youthful idealism and certainty, but that did not seem to exist. When some revolutionaries in the Congo murdered a group of nuns they were holding hostage because their demands weren't met, I asked a radical friend of my parents for his reaction. His discomforting response was that if you made a threat like that, you'd better be prepared to carry it out. I was learning that part of being a dedicated revolutionary was becoming inured to various barbarous acts committed in your name. By the ripe old age of seventeen I found I had outgrown my infatuation with socialism.

While Lenny Glaser could harangue a crowd for hours on end, I completely lacked the ability to discourse on any subject. I wistfully imagined that if I only read enough books, I might achieve the knowledge and understanding to which I aspired. I could rent an apartment, cosset myself within and do nothing but read for a couple of years. There would come a magical moment, a tipping point, when suddenly I would reach critical mass and be able to converse on any subject on the same level as Lenny Glaser, my parents, or anyone else of intellectual substance. I had read about such a thing in Eugene Burdick's novel *The Ninth Wave* where its main character, an aspiring young politician, had done just that.

But that was not meant to be. For one thing, I didn't really enjoy reading. Probably I suffered from ADHD. I couldn't force my eyes to stay locked on the page for long, and then I could barely remember what I'd read. When younger I had read compulsively, forced-marching my way through a series of genres: books about dinosaurs, space travel, Sherlock Holmes, Edgar Allan Poe, H. G. Wells, Jules Verne, Landmark books, *The Black Stallion* series, but now I would rather turn on the radio and listen to my favorite disc jockeys on Top 40 radio. For me, music had become like a drug, an escape from real life, and my drug of choice was the Beatles.

The Beatles were a phenomenon that I found irresistible. The highlight of my summer was attending their August 19 concert at the San Francisco Cow Palace. I rode the bus alone from Berkeley to the Cow Palace and settled into my seat, suffering though a couple of dreary opening acts that generated little reaction from the audience made up almost entirely of teenage girls. When the Beatles appeared, the screams rose to a supersonic pitch, not letting up for the entire performance, drowning out almost completely the sound of the music. The Beatles themselves seemed small and fragile, especially George, who looked to me like a broomstick in his Beatle suit. After their short set was over, the screams subsided to an eerie silence as, completely drained of all emotion, the crowd slowly dissipated.

In the evenings, after Lenny Glaser ended his performance, I would wander down to the campus and watch television in the lounge of the student union building. One evening I was joined by a PhD student in math who sat down next to me and started a conversation. His name was Price, a very conventional-looking Midwesterner from Ohio with a flat top haircut. Of course, he was gay, but I was too innocent to even know what that was about. Probably that innocence both attracted and befuddled him, which was why he never propositioned me. Ironically, I was to become *his* corrupting influence; for a start, he liked the Kingston Trio, but I turned him on to the Beatles. On our first "date" he borrowed a friend's Corvette and we drove to San Francisco to see the movie *The Tenth Victim.* Another time we visited the parents of his friend Vardan, a dashing fellow who was away picking fruit in the Central Valley. His ambition was to own a salmon boat.

Summer came to an end and with the fall began my freshman year. At that time UC had a language requirement and I scored the third highest mark out of six hundred students who took the Spanish placement test. Remarkably, I couldn't speak Spanish, much less understand Fidel's speeches, but after getting my score I marched over to the Dwinelle Hall office of my father, now Chairman of the Philosophy Department, to share the news. This would be the last moment of pride in my accomplishments that we would celebrate for some time.

I had no idea where my academic interests lay and so signed up for a mélange of social science and humanities courses. In one of them we began by reading Dostoevsky's *Notes from Underground.* I identified with this poor soul with a diseased liver, whose overly acute self-consciousness and spiteful nature made him unable to change or do anything but indulge in his own thoughts of self-loathing. But opposed to this spitefulness, he claimed, were swarming in him "many, many opposite elements" craving some outlet, tormenting him to the point of shame, "living in a hell of unsatisfied desires." This was me! How exciting! But this was a small class, and it was obvious we would all be expected to participate in the discussion, a prospect so terrifying that I stopped coming. Cursed with a paralyzing shyness, I feared I would be unable to formulate a coherent thought and my tongue would be tied in knots exposing my inner confusion and shallowness to embarrassment, shame, and ridicule. Eventually I abandoned all my classes, not just because of self-consciousness, but because that October was the outbreak on campus of the famed Free Speech Movement.

University regulations prohibited students from mounting political activity on campus, and the many tables set up in Sproul Plaza by various political groups were in obvious violation. This led to the arrest of campus activist Jack Weinberg who was dragged from his table and loaded in a police car in the plaza. A swarm of students immediately surrounded the car, which remained immobilized for several days with Weinberg trapped inside while a series of speakers, including Mario Savio, exhorted the crowd from the roof of the car. Being part of this idealistic mob was intoxicating, a great movement and crush of humanity united in their opposition to what they saw as the evil University administration. There were almost daily marches, rallies, demonstrations.

At one rally there was talk of occupying Sproul Hall, the administration building, but the doors were locked. Lenny Glaser leapt up crying "to the barricades!" and charged forward trying to break down a door. More sober members of the crowd restrained him. Lenny was too radical for the FSM, and he would wind up going to jail for some of his actions, serving his time alone and forgotten, no longer a charismatic fixture at the entrance to the campus.

Finally, on December 2, after two months of protests, the occupation of Sproul Hall took place as hundreds of students, including Price and me, marched into the building. Inside, the festive atmosphere was broken when inexplicably a group of police entered the building and tried to climb the stairs, clubbing and pushing aside students as they went. Witnessing this scene, I felt outrage and resolved to forever be an outlaw and a revolutionary, having nothing to do with corrupt society. But when the police finally did clear the hall, I cooperated and walked out quietly without "going limp" and having to be dragged out like most of the others.

After spending a night in the Oakland City jail, we were released and returned to the campus as heroes. A large crowd gathered for a rally in Sproul Plaza to hear speeches of support, including from my father. "And I want to welcome everyone back from jail, including my son," he concluded. I stood anonymously in the crowd imagining everyone peering about trying to figure out who exactly was this mysterious son that no one knew. Like the Underground Man, my aloneness was a source of pain and shame, amplified when I happened upon a small group of FSM leaders talking with the folksinger Joan Baez. She had given a couple of concerts at the Greek Theater that summer. Waiting in line for hours to get the best seat in the first row, I had been mesmerized by this lithe beauty with the ethereal voice. Seeing me lurking about she gave me a brief glance. "Who is that stalker?" I imagined her thinking. Perhaps she remembered me sitting rapturously in the front row at the Greek Theater, and later in the crowd as she sang at various FSM rallies. But feeling her inaccessibility, my inability to engage with her or participate in these dramatic events except as a silent and passive observer, was excruciating.

My father was a reluctant supporter of the students. Although he had left wing sympathies and was himself a dedicated advocate of academic freedom and free speech, under his philosophy of education students should adopt an attitude of docility, as the purpose of their education was to initiate them into society and prepare them for the responsibilities of citizenship. He didn't support changes, soon to be implemented across academia, where students were given a role in the running of the institution and the authority of the administration and faculty was eroded. This to him was a perverted version of badly needed academic reform. But he tried his best to straddle the fence.

My father watches as Mario Savio is dragged from the microphone

Once he helped avoid a major confrontation. UC President Clark Kerr had called a campus-wide meeting at the Greek Theater where there was to be a presentation by a committee of faculty composed of the department chairs. My father sat with the other chairmen on stage and as Kerr concluded the meeting Mario Savio jumped up and grabbed the mike. His purpose was simply to announce a counter-meeting to be held at Sproul Plaza, but in a knee-jerk reaction the campus police grabbed him and dragged him backstage where he was locked into a makeshift cell. Marching backstage my father demanded of the nervous guards in an authoritative voice, "Let him go!"—which indeed they did, thereby averting potential disaster. Later he helped shepherd a resolution through the Academic Senate which led to an end to the crisis. Those who were arrested in the sit-in were given token sentences and to this day hold regular reunions reflecting on those times which for many were the most meaningful of their lives. In those heady days it seemed the movement of which we were a part was the beginning of a revolution which would transform society, a hope that would be dashed in the years to come.

By this time my fate was sealed. Had I even cared, by now it would have been impossible to salvage my academic year. That year of the Underground Man and the FSM I received mostly Fs and Incompletes. Expelled from the University for "academic deficiency," I spent an uneventful year attending a local junior college where I met my first girlfriend, a wholesomely normal girl who I helped teach Sunday school at her church. We went out for cheeseburgers at Oscar's, watched movies in the basement of her family home, and once secretly flew to Southern California for the day to visit Disneyland. She must have regarded my innocence as an interesting challenge, which she started chipping away at by giving me badly needed kissing lessons.

After getting reasonable grades, I applied for readmission to Cal for the 1966–67 academic year. "I'll take a plunge and readmit you," announced Dean Fetter of the College of Letters and Science. But that year my grades improved only slightly. My final chance to redeem myself and bring my grade point average up to the required minimum was the summer quarter of 1967, which just happened to coincide with the Summer of Love. For the first time I would be living away from my parents. They would be giving up their rented home on La Vereda Road in the north Berkeley hills and I would be moving into Ehrman Hall, a men's dormitory on the south-side of campus.

I remember the day several months earlier when this move became inevitable. As usual I was ensconced in my room pretending to study but listening instead to Top Forty radio. My father came downstairs from the living room to the bedroom where my mother was reading. There was upsetting news—he was having an affair with a former student and could no longer live with the secret. I could hear my mother's horrifying shrieks as she grabbed a suitcase, stuffed it with a few clothes and flew out the door in a fury.

Her reaction was predictable; she was sensitive and this news hit her like a bolt of lightning. Needing to get away, she left for Portugal where she would live on and off for several years, in between a few abortive attempts to reconcile with my father. Feeling alone and abandoned, she would write to me, although I seldom wrote back.

9 April 1967

Dearest David,

The last few days have been cold and rainy in Cascais. Since I had a small sore throat yesterday, I didn't go swimming. However, I did go the day before. The weather was overcast and the water quite chilly. Nevertheless I enjoyed it once I got in—and I felt marvelous afterwards. I gathered quite an audience (on the esplanade) who, no doubt, thought I was crazy.

There is a *very* nice beach here and the water is nicer than at Santa Barbara, Cascais could very well compare with the latter. It certainly is a lovely resort village with all the advantages. There is sailing here, too—lots of boats for rent.

As for accommodations—I looked at the apartment yesterday and I didn't like it at all. That is, the location was very bad—in the hills behind Cascais. It is part of a new development and the building isn't even finished. I would really be isolated there—and I would prefer living in Lisbon. I am now looking for something else. Rents are higher here, naturally, than in Lisbon, since it is a choice area. I could have a rented place, however, for about $80—the same as in Lisbon. I've seen a few—but I rather like the idea of finding an unfurnished place and furnishing it very simply—from scratch—since the rent is much cheaper. I could sleep on a mattress of *palha*—straw. It doesn't matter.

In the meantime I am staying in a very pleasant pension—inexpensive—where everyone is very nice to me. I can stay as long as I like since there is not much tourist movement at this time.

I am very lonely—especially at night—and after my dinner I go directly to my room. As you might imagine, I feel very sad and I don't know what to do. It seems my whole world has broken.

I hope that you are happy and occasionally studying. Don't waste your time with pop music. It's better to study the guitar. You have so many capacities. I hope you don't betray yourself.

I feel very unhappy when I think of the last memories of me you must have—raging and crying. I never thought that I could behave like that and I am full of despair. Everything has been so terribly ugly and brutal and childish. There is a point at which one can no longer control one's emotions. I am glad that such scenes don't damage you and that you are not so sensitive as I am. That would be insupportable.

I still love you both—but I know that neither of you want me nor need me. Thus, it is very painful that I am so dependent on you two—for love, affection, understanding—for my very life. I don't know if one can remake oneself. If I cannot, then all is finished for me.

I suppose I can never make you understand the need that forced me to leave you both. Certainly it wasn't pleasure. I *had to understand* the world in all its manifestations and dimensions. Some of these dimensions have been destroyed in the U.S. Here one can still see how people have always lived before the machine—and one can thus evaluate better what life is.

I have never needed anyone but you and Joe—but I have deeply needed a greater intellectual experience of life. I was just formed in that way—and no doubt that is a tragic situation for a woman—because she should discover her meaning within her family.

Being such a person as I am, I know that I have failed you in many ways. At the same time there is a compensation for you. I am not a possessive; demanding mother and I only want you to be free and happy. I *would* like to see you more interested in some kind of service to society. However, you will find your own direction.

I did think that I had something to offer Joe being the kind of person I am. But he saw my search as a competitive rather than a complementary one.

I have been too restless and unhappy to make a good wife and good mother. The saddest thing of all is that I have never been capable of doing anything about the misery in the world that has hurt me so much.

Try to remember me with some understanding. No doubt that understanding will only come with experience. One day you might say—"My mother was a very tormented person; one not very well equipped to deal with the world—but she never wanted to hurt anyone." Love,

Lorrie

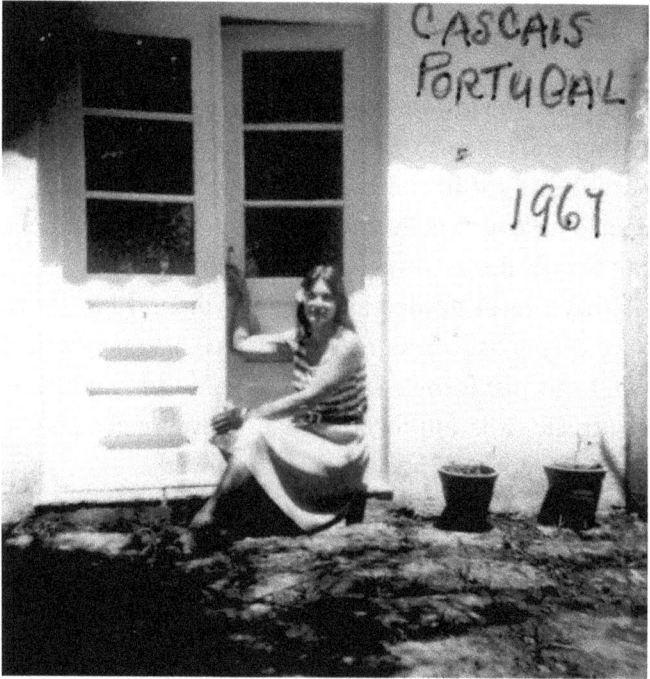

My mother in Cascais, Portugal, 1967

SUMMER OF LOVE

Me in early 1967

Summer of '67, forever immortalized as the Summer of Love! For the first time I was living on my own, in a dormitory a couple blocks from campus. Telegraph Avenue, a mere block away, seemed bright and alive, signs of the counterculture were taking hold. I found myself sitting outdoors at The Forum, a short-lived cafe on the corner of Telegraph and Haste, with the two most beautiful and hip women from the dorms, Pat O'Neil, a perky short-haired brunette, and Linda Benson, a dark-haired soulful siren, thinking this was going to be a spectacular summer.

It was only a matter of days after moving in that I met Roland. He invited me up to his room, pulled a suitcase out from under his bed, and opened it to reveal a still-wrapped kilo of marijuana. It was the first time I had seen pot, much less smoked any, and my eyes must have bugged out of my head. Roland had just driven back from Tijuana with the kilo hidden under his car seat, he claimed. He was a low-key dealer who sold lids—one-ounce baggies—to a select clientele. I regarded him as the coolest person I had ever met. He hung out with black guys playing pool in San Francisco, then would head over to North Beach for an extravagant five-dollar dinner, an unbridled hedonist who enjoyed women and all the finer things of life. I shared a joint with him, never admitting it was my first one, and we headed up Telegraph Avenue towards Pizza Haven. To my amazement we were having an animated conversation, Roland complementing me on my wit and intelligence.

On the way the effects of the pot hit me with full force. Looking up at the evening sky I perceived an angelic image of my mother gazing down at me with a benevolent expression, but as I looked her figure morphed into that of a malevolent witch riding on a broomstick, her face twisted and pained. I tried my best to put this disturbing image out of my mind, but it perfectly expressed my ambivalent feelings about her.

Arriving back at the dorm we encountered a beautiful blonde freshman from Los Angeles named Layla sitting on the grass in front of the dorm. In violation of dorm rules Roland invited her up to his room where we smoked more pot and chatted. Roland had stolen one of those red flashing lights from a construction site and it provided suitable ambiance for the occasion. Getting out of the elevator as we escorted Layla back to her room, she looked at me and proclaimed, "I knew you were a head the minute I saw you!" I must be a quick study, for I had only just become a head that same evening.

Roland and I were to have a falling out over Layla, and as a result my summer was pretty much a disaster. For it was fated that a couple of days later Layla and I ran into each other in Sproul Plaza listening to a lunch hour concert. Between songs it was announced there was to be a Banjo and Fiddle Contest in Topanga Canyon near Los Angeles in a couple of weeks. "Let's go!" we agreed. That evening the Chambers Brothers played a concert in Pauley Ballroom and of course we went. In the back of my mind there was something forbidden about Layla; was she not really Roland's girl? After all, it was he who had made the first move. But never mind. After the concert we drove up to my parents' house on La Vereda where we spent the night, platonically, sleeping on the sofa in the living room. In the morning my father came upstairs and very cheerfully made us breakfast. "Why is your dad being so cool?" Layla asked. Probably he was equally enchanted by her beauty, or maybe he was feeling relief that perhaps there was hope his son might be normal after all.

Only a few days later my father moved out of the house into a room at the Faculty Club on campus. So the house was sitting empty when Layla and I decided to walk up there one gorgeous afternoon. As we ambled along hand in hand we marveled at the magical summer day, the butterflies and buttercups, the wispy white clouds in the sky, the birds happily singing in the trees. My father had left a fold-up bed on the deck outside and that is where we wound up spending the night, making love for the first time. I cannot know what she thought of this experience, but I certainly gave it my best effort. Her naked body in the bathtub the next morning was the most beautiful sight I had ever seen.

Layla and I carried through on our whimsical plan to go to the Banjo and Fiddle Contest. We drove down in the old Peugeot 404 that my father had handed down, joined by

Layla's brother and his lovely girlfriend. Her brother was a grad student in biochemistry, a serious substantial type who when we met looked me over with an air of puzzlement that I pretended not to notice. I fit in no better with the rest of her family in Los Angeles. Her brother had long discussions with their father about his activities in the Peace and Freedom Party while I sat silently listening. Layla and her mother had painful discussions regarding her sexually active lifestyle. We accompanied a second brother to the hospital where his toddler son was isolated in a room suspended from the ceiling in some awful contraption while he recovered from a recent hip injury. But Layla and I had no discussions about anything. It seemed that once the first blush of magic had worn off I could think of nothing to talk about. An old high school friend of Layla's came by and we went on a walk. I listened as they talked about some issue his father was having. I wondered, "Is that all they can think of to talk about? Surely there must be something more interesting." But at least they were talking about something.

On our return to Berkeley, driving down Telegraph Avenue Layla calmly turned to me and said, "I don't want to date seriously anymore."

"Oh, okay," I meekly replied. Hardly my own best advocate, I was unable to mount any argument to the contrary.

Later I gathered my courage and went up to Roland's room on the eighth floor. He was with a friend named Greg, my replacement, who he was trying to convince to go on a double date with some loose girls he had met. "What's in it for me?" Greg asked.

"A poke," Roland replied matter-of-factly. Greg consented to the arrangement and left.

"I hope you're not upset about what happened with Layla," I said apologetically.

"Oh no, Roland replied, "It takes a lot more than that to get me pissed off." I wasn't convinced. "But I knew you'd fuck up, so I just had to wait until you did."

That was the last time I would ever speak to Roland, and sure enough, a few days later when returning to the dorm I spotted Layla and Roland locked in a passionate embrace in the moonlit courtyard by the dining hall.

So much for my Summer of Love. I smoked a lot of pot, wandering aimlessly around Berkeley in a cloud of depression. I wanted to be a hippie, purchasing some love beads at a head shop on Telegraph Avenue, but when I showed up for dinner at the dorm, Miriam Puckett took one look at me and exclaimed, "You're no hippie!" Of course, she was right.

On weekends I would head over to the Fillmore auditorium and listen raptly—and stoned—to the likes of The Who, Cream, Jimi Hendrix, Janis Joplin, Jefferson Airplane, the Dead, Quicksilver, and the Doors. Jim Morrison of the Doors made a deep impression with his tousled hair, classic chiseled features and contemptuous attitude. Dressed in black leather pants and a white flowing shirt he would stumble and flail about the stage, seemingly drunk or stoned or both. Or was it all part of the act? Once after being laughed at by some frat boys in the audience, he stopped and defiantly cried, "You can laugh all you want, but I'm the one who's up here *doing* it!" Another time I went with a group from the dorms that included Linda Benson, who claimed she had once dated Morrison. She went backstage but came back hurt and confused, explaining that he had just sat there with a blank look, not even acknowledging her.

Distracted and despondent, I had no interest in attending any classes, with one exception. I had signed up for Psych 150, a class in Personality Psychology taught by a kindly, bearded gentleman named Bill Soskin. Personality theory intrigued me. Perhaps it might explain what was wrong with me. But the real appeal of his course was the Monday morning class where he would regale us with accounts of the LSD trips he had taken over the weekend. I had heard of LSD, I'm not sure where, sometime in the year when I attended junior college. I had even bought a copy of the book *Varieties of Psychedelic Experience* which I proudly carried around with me, although I never actually read it. But Soskin's accounts were riveting. Not only did the trips sound like an amazing visual experience, but through them could be gained deep transformative insight. And it could be done all by yourself, perfect for an introvert like me!

Soskin's class further introduced me to the study of psychohistory. Not only could psychological analysis unlock the mysteries of one's personality, but it could explain the entire course of human history through its analysis of historical figures and trends! We were assigned the book *Young Man Luther,* in which author Erik Ericson described the twenties of Martin Luther as a period of "psychosocial moratorium" during which he went through a profound identity crisis, searching for his place in society. This not only perfectly described my current status of disengagement but tended to rationalize and even glorify it.

I wanted to become a psychohistorian, but such analysis would become unfashionable, as it was more and more accepted that history and society must be analyzed through the lens of power, gender, race, and class—subjects that bored me immensely.

One day during the summer I ventured down to Palo Alto to visit Laurel. She was a friend of my cousin, a Berkeley student who was spending the summer at home with her parents. I had met her that spring and had developed a serious but unrequited crush, to the point that she was virtually all I ever thought about. Every day I would stand on the steps of the Student Union waiting for her to walk by on her way to class, running up to her like an eager little puppy. But that summer she invited me down for a visit. I drove up to her house in my Peugeot where her father was working on something in his garage. She had described him as a real mensch, putting him in a different class from me. He gave me the standard quizzical look, and Laurel and I wandered off to stroll the Stanford campus. She asked why I was smoking so much pot, and I responded that when stoned I experienced wonderful groovy images. She appeared frustrated that I was not able to describe them in any more detail, but I assured her that they were indeed groovy.

That evening a couple of friends of hers came over. We smoked some pot and drove around Palo Alto, Laurel and I cozy in the back seat. She sighed, and it seemed for a moment she was about to share something personal, for the first time taking me seriously as a friend. But I felt uneasy, as if her neediness and vulnerability were about to expose the emptiness inside of me. I glanced over and to my horror, her face had morphed into something scary, unattractive, even repulsive, just as had occurred with my mother on my first pot trip! That was the end of my infatuation with Laurel.

The last day of the summer quarter was bittersweet. I bade goodbye to my roommate, whom I had barely interacted with all summer. "Stay in touch," I said absentmindedly as he got in his parents' car. "Yeah, sure!" was the sarcastic response.

I went upstairs, propped my speaker in the window facing outward to the courtyard and blasted Jimi Hendrix playing "Purple Haze" as loud as I could. The house mother was perturbed but it was too late for any disciplinary action. The next day I moved out, putting everything into the back of my Peugeot and sleeping overnight in the car, for I had no place to go. I managed to rent a room in a boarding house at the corner of Blake and Chilton just off Telegraph where the finality of my situation sank in. Word came swiftly: I had failed to improve my grade point average and for the second time was expelled for academic deficiency. I was not devastated. In fact, thanks to *Young Man Luther,* I was quite elated. To my father I enthused, "This could be the best thing that ever happened to me!" My psychosocial moratorium was about to kick into high gear.

THE BROKEN ARCH

My upstairs corner room on Chilton Way was simply furnished with a bed and chair, my hi-fi and colorful bedspreads for curtains. My mother, back from Portugal, paid me a visit. I'm sure she noticed, but didn't mention, the acrid smell of marijuana that filled the house. "Do you think it's the gout medication that is causing Joe to behave the way he is?" she asked, referring to my father's ongoing affair.

"No," I said. That suggestion was ridiculous to me, as were many of my mother's ideas. "Maybe Joe is happy," I ventured. Clearly shaken by my betrayal, my mother sputtered a little, cutting her visit short. How to connect with this horrible son who was not only taking his father's side but was siding with his mistress against her! That terrible woman, as she referred to her, was making Joe happy! Was I even conscious of the depth of the betrayal contained in that casual statement?

I had been well-groomed for the betrayal. Julia was only a couple years older than me, a beautiful and charming grad student in political science, a transfer from Harvard where Henry Kissinger had been her advisor. After my mother departed for Portugal, Julia became a regular visitor to our house, making my father and I dinners featuring her delicious shrimp salad. Once she invited me out for ice cream and on the way, she told me she loved me. "I hope that doesn't embarrass you," she said. It did. No one had ever said that before. Sometimes she would talk about my mother. There is darkness at her core, she professed. She was not a loving, kind person, and she certainly was not a good mother. She accused her of abusing me because one night years before we had shared a bed at a motel in Santa Barbara. I read her a paper I wrote on Plato's *Symposium,* which she claimed impressed her greatly. I would never share anything like that with my mother, knowing that inwardly her response would be judgmental. Of course Julia made my father happy. The two of them were soul mates, she proclaimed.

One evening after finishing our shrimp salad Julia turned to me and asked, "David, what's it like for you being an undergraduate at Berkeley during these times?"

"Well," I replied, "it's great to be at the center of things, Berkeley is where it's at, it's where it's all happening right now." Inwardly I cringed. I couldn't believe I was spouting such drivel, especially in front of my father, who thankfully kept his thoughts to himself. When I had returned home from my night in jail after my FSM arrest, I had the sense that my parents' sincere but condescending reaction was *Oh how cute, our little boy is a political activist now!* What made it worse was that it wasn't even me. I was no activist; for me it was all just entertainment, relief from the boredom of student life. My commitment to political activism quickly faded after the FSM, as the student movement lost its innocence and idealism. Where the FSM has been peaceful and non-violent, anarchy and violence would soon take over during the protests over the Vietnam War and Peoples Park. Regular trashings of Telegraph Avenue would turn the area into a war zone. When Black Panther Eldredge Cleaver, speaking at the Berkeley Community Theater, called for the destruction of Western Civilization, to my dismay his privileged white middle class audience cheered wildly. As for me, this was not a project I cared to be a part of.

My mother on the beach at Cascais, Portugal, 1969

Despite her charms, Julia was no competition for my mother in beauty or intelligence. Now in her forties and no longer entertaining ideas of a future in academia, my mother was still a legendary presence on campus. She had a daily routine, showing up at the Café Espresso (known derogatorily as Café Depresso) on Hearst Avenue and taking the table in the window to review her correspondence, always wearing a fresh flower in her hair. Every day she would receive letters from all over the world. There was Tomas from Portugal, a young student who for years wrote daily until he died of testicular cancer. There was Pierre Emmanuel, a French poet who came to Portugal trying, unsuccessfully, to find her, settling instead for dedicating a poem to her. Then there was Mostafa, an Iranian economist and diplomat, who she met when he was a graduate student at Syracuse.

June 4, 1959, he would write from Washington, D.C:

l wish l could enjoy your very charming company. l
have had many friends in this country and abroad, but
none has impressed me as much as you have done. As l
have told you often you are unique and not seeing you
is a great loss to me which cannot be compensated by
anyone else. l just don't know what to say and how to
leave this country without even the hope of seeing you
again. Could you give me any hope?

September 16, 1960, from Tehran:

It is more than a year that l haven't seen you, and yet—to
be quite frank—l love you more than ever. l think there
is no sin in admitting to a dear friend what goes within
your mind and heart. But could l have any hopes or you
are completely out of reach?

February 1, 1961, from Milan:

Lorrie, let me be very frank with you. l am deeply in love
with you and l am saying this after testing myself for
a period of two years. But am l loving someone who is
completely out of reach or is there any hope?

October 21, 1961, from Tehran:

l was wondering whether you would consider the pos-
sibility of coming to Iran as my dearest guest or at least
accept a job with the Economic Bureau here...Lorrie, it
would be so wonderful to see you in Iran. You can bring

David. There is a good American school and there are good dentists too. Tennis is also played here.

December 9, 1961, from Tehran:

...last August I took the trip from Wash D.C. to S.F. so as to come to Santa Barbara to see you. That was pretty close and yet it couldn't be done. Frankly I was very much annoyed when you turned me down. If friendship means anything, it does mean that much that one can sacrifice a day for a friend who has come such a long way...I have never seen any girl as beautiful and as erudite as you with so much charm and other qualities. But let me add, if I may, that, as you say, your feeling of suspense between guilts has robbed you of any decision of life...

My translation of Gibran's *Prophet* will be published late this month. Just an hour ago I did the proof reading of the last page. I am quoting this from the English version for you:

If in the twilight of memory we
Should meet once more, we shall
Speak again together and you shall
Sing to me a deeper song.
And if our hands should meet in
Another dream we shall build
Another tower in the sky.

Mostafa was but one of many suitors who would never build that tower in the sky. But at the Café Depresso, they would line up daily to wait their turn to join her at the window table. Americans did not interest her; it was only foreign students who could capture her attention. They would discuss the politics of their home countries and my mother would share her ideas about all that was wrong with the world, what she described as the broken architecture of the cosmos.

In my senior year of high school, I volunteered to type the manuscript that distilled those ideas into her unpublished work entitled *The Broken Arch*. It began,

> "My life is a broken arch," Henry Adams wrote at the beginning of this century. And today Jean-Paul Sartre writes these words in an essay about the art of Giacometti:
>
> > Between things as between man, the bridges are broken, and emptiness seeps in everywhere, every creature concealing his own.
>
> Sartre sees Giacometti struggling with the problem of the insuperable distances and solitudes between objects and individuals as a result of the broken architecture of the cosmos...
>
> The problem of Giacometti is essentially the problem of creation without perspective. How is the artist to define an object that exists only in itself...an object without connections, without external relationships... form not in relationship to other forms and to space, but form *en vacuo?* In other words, how is the artist to define that which is free?
>
> The paradox is not only one of art but in the widest sense of life itself. How are we to define either ourselves or others if we are freed from our traditional contexts and connections? How are we to understand life itself without a common perspective?

We have sought to escape the center of our cosmos... that rock, shrine or temple that revealed to us a unifying vision of experience. At some point in our history we reversed our direction. We became pioneers instead of pilgrims—expanding and redefining the contours of the world, opening horizons, converting our boundaries into frontiers. It is from those ever-shifting frontiers that we have attempted to derive our perspective. But now we find that we have lost focus. The cosmos has disappeared in a confusion of dissolving views and we no longer are able to form a unified image of what we see...

But must we abandon perspective, reject form, desert Apollo for Dionysus—seeking understanding, if at all, not through reason, but through any means of heightened or mystical sensation available to us? Must we artificially invoke an inner vision in order to grasp our disintegrating universe? We have sought to experience the world directly, discarding the parables that helped us to interpret our experience, discarding the miracles of faith that enabled us to act. But in substituting reality for religion we find that it has "taken away from us even what we hath."

Inspired by the ideas of Henry Adams, my mother defined the problem in terms of the struggle between God, who is unity, and the devil, who is complexity.

What now passes for unity in the modern world is really the imposition of a common meaningless pattern upon all men and all societies; the metamorphosis of traditionally diverse cultures into a "monoculture;" the transformation of the world into a frontier that leads nowhere—that denies both Cosmos and Chaos. What passes for multiplicity, complexity, diversity, is really confusion...

But, as Henry Adams realized when he called himself "the Virgin's pilgrim," the medieval church possessed a mysterious relationship, an image that protected it for a while from destruction—by an omnipotent Lutheran God, by prodigal sons and Homeric heroes escaping from boundaries, by pioneers seeking frontiers, by logicians seeking "reality" rather than truth. That image was Gaia reincarnated as the Virgin Mary who maintained the connections, the structural equilibrium, until she was defeated by the dynamo that turned the image into process, freedom into a boundary, the part into the whole...

It is not God who is dead. He still survives as an ideal for the self. It is actually Mary, the maternal principle, nature, that is dead.

My mother's horror at the counterculture was revealed in an article she wrote for the French journal *Preuves:*

A few years ago a college generation was profoundly moved by a novel by Albert Camus, *L'Étranger.* It seemed to express the alienation of youth from society, an alienation that had its roots not in ideas and ideals, but, negatively, in a total lack of emotional and intellectual response to the conventional social structures. *L'Étranger* is a parable. In the opening lines lies the clue to our condition. In the last few years there are new spokesmen for youth, but none who have responded to that clue.

Unfortunately, this "spirit of youth" is fundamentally

negative and destructive since it springs from the modern radical situation of the breakdown of unity. Historically there have been breakdowns in the beliefs of an age, in the organizing principles of a civilization; but never until recently the sophisticated, desperate and thorough attack on belief itself that is now paralyzing traditional structures of thought and action, communication and organization...

The picture presented by the modern world is one of explosive liberation from the traditional controls of nature and society. We are essentially free from all tyrannies. But our confusion, hesitation, purposelessness mark us not as free men, but as slaves. Freedom has ironically set up its own unique categories of limitation more profound and disturbing than those from which we have struggled to free ourselves. The Crowd, the Monoculture, on the one hand, and the Alienated Individual on the other, are manifestations of this new tyranny...

The consequences are most tragic on the level of youth. While we have been driven to "embrace our paradox." to exist within our "free society," carrying on our "piecemeal engineering" and making our compromise decisions, young people are reacting blindly, explosively, and intensely. They are reacting to a world condition without any significant basis from which they can understand, condemn and correct that condition...

"Aujourd'hui maman est morte" (Today mother is dead)—those crucial opening lines of Camus's L'Étranger—is a statement of fact, both personal and immediate, universal and historical. Youth couldn't care less since they don't see the connection between that death and their alienation. God is dead today because Mary is dead. This all has its origin in the time of the Greeks when Gaia, the Earth, was sacrificed for Odysseus—who was, in effect, Ouranos, the god of the boundary in the guise of the wanderer.

Modern man has rejected the notion of a cosmos governed by a unifying principle. By so doing, he has denied the cosmos itself. Actually, he lives today in the condition that the Greeks named "ouranos," the boundary, the area of change and becoming. He is freed from his relationship with the natural world and possesses no external framework by which to measure or define himself. Youth, desperately needing unity and lacking the guidance of the older generation, cannot be blamed for following anti-heroes and false prophets; for attempting to destroy the final distinctions between natural and artificial, male and female, form and freedom.

"Yes," my mother would write to her own mother,

we are living in a time of revolution. The trouble is that no one really understands that revolution or has any idea about how to direct it or how to create a better society in place of the old mess. The young people are rebelling against the mindless, spiritually and physically empty consumer-machine society that we have developed—but they are so lost—trying to escape into drugs and sex.

LSD

For me, as an incurable introvert, drugs and sex had a particularly heady appeal. Freed of all responsibilities, I now threw myself headlong into the pursuit of both. In the world of the counterculture there were two classes of culture heroes: rock stars and drug dealers. I had no musical talent, so the choice was obvious. I wanted to be, like Roland, a drug dealer. The allure of living a secret underground life, of illicit drugs and money, intoxicated me. My parents had been intellectuals, interested only in ideas. For them money was little but a crass inconvenience, something one dared hardly speak of, which made it even more enticing. But I needed a source, and oddly enough the Bay Area was going through a dry spell. Scoring a kilo of grass was proving very difficult, and, unlike Roland, I was not about to drive to Tijuana. But I persisted, pursuing one lead after another to no avail.

When not trying to score I settled into the lobby of the Spens-Black women's dormitory as my second home. Like the potted plant next to the elevator, I became a permanent fixture, observing one beautiful female student after another going in and out. I must have been viewed as something of an oddity, but nonetheless I became friendly with several of them. There was Barbara, with her striking long red hair, dressed always in blue jeans and a blue work shirt, no makeup, arriving in Berkeley from boarding school in Switzerland. Quiet

and introverted like me, I was so much in awe that I dared
not even touch her, but we went to the Fillmore Auditorium
and listened to music together. There was Susan, a lovely psychology student from the Midwest who seemed to like me.
We went out for meals occasionally and went to Winterland
to see Donovan, whose music and persona was the ultimate
expression of flower power. When my hair became just a bit
too long she gave me a haircut. There was Alida, a high school
classmate of Layla, a sweet but too trusting girl whose body
was to be found in a shallow grave in Tilden Park. And there
was Edith, a passionate object of my desire. We spent a heav-
enly night in my little room kissing, and I begged ten dollars
from my father so I could take her out for a Mexican dinner
at La Fiesta and a banana split at Edy's. That indulgence was
the last I would see of her.

Alone in my hippie pad I would smoke pot and listen to
records at all hours. Strangely, none of the other tenants
complained. I can't recall ever meeting any of them. I didn't
like to smoke pot around others, it made me even more
withdrawn and depressed. If in a group that was similarly
stoned, it wouldn't be long before I would want to leave, yet I
would be too afraid to speak up even to say goodbye. But I did
enjoy listening to music. I would lose myself in the music, it
would slow down, I would savor every note, each song would
become a long journey creating in my head those dreamlike,
groovy images I found so compelling.

In the shared bathroom I would gaze at myself in the
mirror. My face seemed young, blank, featureless, lacking
in character or gravitas. This concerned me because if I was
to be a drug dealer, I needed to project a certain amount
of charisma, to look like someone who was a "heavy." But
nonetheless I persisted and eventually succeeded in scoring
my first kilo—enough for thirty-five one ounce "lids" which

I would sell at eight dollars each, almost tripling my initial investment.

It seemed I had a ready-made clientele. Residents of my summer dorm had spread out and colonized other dorms. Some were consumers, some would become dealers themselves. There were the girls of Spens-Black. There was Jim, an acquaintance of Roland, who was also dabbling in dealing. There was Chris and John, two personable freshmen who had furnished the ultimate hippie pad on Dana Street not far from me and also aspired to become dealers. There was Deke and his crew, who now occupied an apartment behind the Top Dog on Durant where one could enjoy hotdogs from Nathans.

My marketing approach was the opposite of cool, unlike Roland. I would pack a small suitcase and stride up and down the halls of the men's dorms calling out, "Lids! Lids!" I almost begged to be noticed, to be recognized for my notoriety. Girls from Spens-Black would sometimes ask for bennies (speed pills) to help them study, which I would get them as a favor, but they never bought lids.

As 1967 came to a close I decided some changes were in order. My dealing was generating a modest income, which I decided to supplement by getting a job as a letter carrier, perfect cover for my other occupation. I found a new friend named Paul and we decided to move into a shared apartment. We found a two-bedroom place on Channing Way that was occupied by an engineering student named Mike who needed new roommates. Unlike Berkeley's funky old brown shingles, this was a modern apartment, already furnished with bunk beds for Paul and me in the second bedroom. Obtaining consent from the landlord, we moved in just before Christmas, while Mike was away for the holidays. With the new Master Card I had received unsolicited from my bank I went out and purchased a fancy stereo. I was all set for my new life.

I had just managed to score a kilo of pot and so alone in the apartment I set about breaking it down into lids. I had also scored my first tablet of LSD and decided it was a good time to try it. Thus, my first experience on acid was the difficult task of focusing my attention on separating the seeds and stems from the buds of marijuana on the kitchen counter. While doing this I noticed the walls were dissolving into swirling psychedelic patterns. I put Jimi Hendrix on the stereo and was enraptured by the ethereal sounds of his soaring guitar. I looked out the window, and the nighttime stars—the whole sky—were exploding like fireworks. I went up to the roof to take it all in, marveling at the brilliant lightshow. It seemed to herald a new beginning, a rebirth. I felt a surge of well-being, of optimism for the future. Life was going to be great! Then back to the kitchen to continue cleaning the grass.

Then back up to the roof! Huddled next to the doorway I encountered another tenant. He was not up there to watch the lightshow but had been in a fight with his girlfriend and had stormed out, telling her he was going to San Francisco to have a good time. Instead, there he was, cold and alone on the roof. I felt sorry for him but didn't let it interfere with my reverie.

The following week of Christmas vacation was a bit of debauchery. A hippie friend of Paul visited and wound up sleeping in Mike's bed. Seeds and stems were still strewn all about the kitchen along with uneaten food and its wrappings. The apartment was a disorganized mess when Mike returned a day early to find a stranger in his bed.

Mike was a solid sort of guy who had no interest in a hippie lifestyle. Coincidentally, my grandmother who lived in Santa Monica had once mentioned to me that she knew a girl from Los Angeles who was attending Berkeley. She was smart, serious, and attractive, I was told, someone I should consider dating. But, lo and behold, she was already dating Mike! Through the thin wall that separated our bedrooms I could hear her moaning his name as they made love. No one would ever moan like that for me.

Mike quickly made plans to vacate the apartment, a wise decision on his part. We found a substitute roommate named Alex, someone more in tune with our alternative lifestyle. I began my job at the post office, earning two dollars and eighty-five cents an hour, stumbling out of bed at five-thirty in the morning still clouded by the effects of the previous night's pot smoking, and in the evenings, I would make the rounds of my drug dealing friends or hang out at my apartment.

By chance I ran into my friend Price who I hadn't seen in some time. He must have been surprised at the course my life had taken since he met me as an innocent freshman. I had hardly seemed like someone who would flunk out of school and become a drug dealer. When I told him about my first LSD trip, he casually mentioned that he knew someone I should meet. His name was Ben.

Ben lived in an old brown shingle house next to the Seven Palms market on the north side of campus, not far from Price. He was a dealer in psychedelics, mainly LSD, and Price introduced me as a potential new distributor of his product. He seemed to like me, saying I looked hip without being so outrageous as to attract attention—a good attitude for a dealer, he said. Ben claimed—whether true or not, I had no idea—that he had a source from a Canadian acid lab and that the acid was laced with a compound that would prevent it from testing positive by the narks. Ben was friendly and genuine, not at all a fast-talking shyster as many dealers would prove to be. He was a good connection, and I could score acid for less than anyone I knew, so it made sense to give up selling

lids and focus on the more lucrative psychedelic market. I
started selling small amounts which would slowly escalate to
larger amounts.

It was while waiting in the anteroom at Ben's apartment
one afternoon that I first encountered Juan seated across
from me also waiting for an audience with Ben. I sat uncomfortably, not knowing what to say, soon to realize that he was
the embodiment of the intellect, style, charisma, and charm
that I lacked. Juan's grandfather had been the last republican
prime minister of Spain before the Civil War that would send
him into exile, first in London and then in Paris. There he
raised Juan and his sister in an apartment in the sixteenth
arrondissement where Pablo Picasso and Maria Callas paid
visits. Upon the death of his grandfather, Juan moved to
Mexico City where he finished high school and was admitted
to Yale with a self-created double major in surrealism and
existentialism. There he started a left-wing faction of the
debating society, arguing with the less radical John Kerry and
others.

Just before graduation from Yale, Juan read an article about
LSD. Being passionately opposed to the Vietnam War, he
was impressed with the assertion that LSD could transform
people's consciousness and turn them against the war. He
decided he had to come to California to find Owsley, who the
article identified as the leading underground source of acid.
Arriving in San Francisco, wandering the streets of the Haight
Ashbury, he met some locals who invited him to crash at their
place. Unfortunately, their place was raided that night and
Juan wound up in jail. As a result, he never graduated from
Yale, and although he never found Owsley, he remained in
the Bay Area where he quickly became a unique figure in the
psychedelic underground. He spoke fluent French, Spanish,
and English with an aristocratic accent, smoked French

cigarettes, and was always surrounded by beautiful women who would chauffeur him around in his green Porsche, he himself lacking a driver's license. After serving his time in jail resulting from his unfortunate bust, he connected with Ben and thus wound up in the waiting room looking me over, although we were not then to exchange any words.

One day my roommate Paul showed up at our apartment with a new girlfriend named Cassie. I didn't like her. She seemed dull and empty-headed, but maybe I was just jealous that I didn't have a girlfriend. If I had a girlfriend, I fantasized, she would be my assistant following me around with a little notebook keeping track of my drug transactions.

I asked Cassie what she was studying, and she revealed she was in an experimental program. "The Tussman Program?" I casually inquired, referring to my father's program by its popular name.

The Experimental Collegiate Program, as it was formally called, was not, as many assumed, in the style of the many "free universities" that sprang up in the wake of student protests. In fact, its inspiration was derived from an experimental college started by Alexander Meiklejohn, my father's mentor, at the University of Wisconsin in the 1930s. The idea was a radical restructuring of the first two years of undergraduate education. In my father's own words,

> I start with the wonderfully baffling idea that liberal education is education for the ruling function, and the companion conviction that since everyone in a democracy is to share in the ruling function, everyone needs to

share in the education reserved, in elitist societies, for the ruling class...

The freshman and sophomore years, the lower division, is generally the wasteland of American higher education...The Program idea was to take the conception of liberal education as broadly politically vocational and insert it into the spiritually empty lower division years—thus filling a deep but unfelt need while at the same time giving a significant point to an otherwise pointless phase of American college education.

...[It was an attempt to] achieve something of a working intellectual community—a group of faculty and students engaged in a common enterprise, creating a structure of ritual and habit triumphant over the impulses of disintegration—an intellectual community as a way of life, sustained for a significant period of time.

There would be no courses or grades, but rather students and faculty would immerse themselves in a common curriculum, starting with reading the *Iliad*, through small seminars, group meetings, and regular writing assignments. They would continue reading great works from four critical periods in Western Civilization through present day, but it was not a "great books" program. Rather, it was an

attempt to provide for our present crises the cultural context within which they are to be understood. Something has happened when you can grasp the thread that runs from Orestes and Antigone to West *Virginia v Barnette* and the Presidential campaign of 1988. When you can see that the attempt to impose the Tablets of the Law upon the worshippers of the Golden Calf is the same struggle as is involved in our attempts to make the

Constitutional Covenant and the Law prevail over our hedonic impulses and narrow partialities. The failure to provide this great context is to send our students, robbed of their proper clothing, of their proper minds, naked into the jabbering world.

All did not go smoothly. Professors who were recruited for the first two-year program were out of place trying to fit into a collegial environment, used to being master of the discrete courses which they usually taught.

But the teacher, the aspiring great teacher, is, in a perverted version, the seducer, the enchanter working his magic on a concrete local group. He must capture it, or he is nothing. He does not like to share the limelight; the presence of fellow professionals is intrusive and distracting; he is best at a one-man show; he worries about being upstaged or outshone. I think the conception of teaching as a "performing art" is deeply mistaken, but it is quite popular. And it makes cooperative teaching almost impossible.

A group of graduate students hired as "teaching assistants" had their own ideas about educational reform, ultimately leading my father to adopt a position he neither sought nor wanted—that of authoritarian decision maker for the group. His first unilateral decision was to fire the teaching assistants, an unpopular move that would lead students like Cassie to question his authority.

And finally, there was the issue of the house itself, which had been taken over by various hangers-on who shared no interest in the vision of the program.

There was the House. It was obvious that some sort of physical center was needed. If students were to interact in a common program there had to be someplace for them to meet. Space was scarce...In the end we considered ourselves lucky to be able to capture an abandoned fraternity house on the edge of the campus, and it was patched up and sparsely furnished for our use. Rooms were fixed up as offices for the faculty, a few as seminar rooms. There was a Program office, a large reading room, a great hall. Not lavish, but adequate. I suppose it was because I began with such high hopes that I came to detest the very sight of it. I had dreamed that it would be the lively center of our life, a place you could drop in to at any time and find students and faculty working and talking...Well, I am not, a quarter of a century later, going to allow myself to feel again the disgust at the ugly culture that came to dominate and to mock the university conception of civilization. What should have been part of an adult university became a juvenile counter-culture hangout. I felt responsible for the existence of the House and felt guilty at my betrayal of my university colleagues who had trusted me to conduct, in their name, an experiment in liberal education.

Only a vigorous imagination can begin to grasp the enormity of trying to initiate the class of sixty-something into an ongoing American branch of western civilization. They gave us a house to try it in. It was the battleground, but I'm not sure everyone recognized what the battle was all about. It was to see whether our traditional cultural resources were powerful enough to withstand the contemptuous challenge of a despairing counterculture. I suppose that sounds grandiose. I think back to the House in its seedy disarray, half deserted, a

handful of disgruntled students arriving for a dispirited
seminar, or, again, to an argumentative throng, unexpectedly cheerful about something or other—a confus-
ing sequence of disordered scenes. I am reminded of the
scene in which Stendhal's hero, galloping away from
a trivial bit of confusion, pauses and wonders, "Was
that the battle of Waterloo?" So, I ask myself, having
crept away, was that really a battle in the war over the
American soul? Without banners? Without a band? Yes,
it was. Sometimes it seemed as if the world was struggling to turn itself into illustrative material to accompany the core curriculum of the Experimental Program.
We were dealing, of course, with the themes that swirled
about one of our greatest achievements —the creation
and development of the great art of Politics. To begin
with the *Iliad* is to begin in medias res, in the midst of
the perpetual war between the Human Expedition and
the Human City, between the Quest and the Home. The
tale is echoed or mimicked in the masterful account of
the war to the death between Athens and Sparta, the par-
adigmatic cultures of the marketplace and the barracks,
of freedom and of discipline. Against that background
we grapple with the conflicting claims of Olympian
rationality and Dionysian passion, with the elevation
of Law over Fury, with the defiance of Law in the name
of the Higher Law, with the great Platonic depiction of
the parallel between Psyche and Polity ranging from the
achievement of Wisdom to the reign of anarchy and tyranny in each. And then in the other of our great moods
we contemplate the Covenant in the Wilderness on
the road from Slavery to dreams of freedom, and ring
a different set of changes on the problems of Authority,
Obedience, Rebellion, War and Peace, Justice, Laws and

Courts. And in the end, we come to see ourselves, to find ourselves, to know ourselves, as the present act in an ancient and perpetual drama...

The converted fraternity house that served as the home of
The Tussman Program

The other day as I drove by [the house], a small drama from the past popped into my mind. I had walked in at about 7 AM. No one was there. I looked with distaste at the disorder, the weary furniture, the carelessly strewn objects. Then I stared in irritation at the enormous poster, the head of Dylan (Bob, not Thomas), lording confidently over the great hall. Unavoidable, dominating. It had annoyed me for weeks. On a reckless impulse I stood on a chair, unpinned the poster, rolled it up and carried it off to my office. Some hours later an indignant young man stomped in. "What happened to my picture?" I looked at him coolly. "I took it down." "Why did you take it down?" It was not really a question. I parried with, "Why did you put it up?" "I put it up," he said, contemptuous in advance of an assertion of authority, "because I felt like it!" "I took it down," I said, "because

I felt like it." He stood silent for a rather long moment. Finally he nodded. "Fair enough," he acknowledged, reached for his poster, and left with the head of Dylan under his arm. Whim baffles whim. The memory of that small triumph of reason warms me.

Sadly, after four years and two groups of one hundred and fifty students each, my father abandoned efforts to continue the program.

In the end, the Program must be judged to have made no enduring difference to the quality of education at Berkeley. The sea of normal life has closed over the sunken hope, the surface now unbroken, the depths unvisited.

"So, what do you think of Professor Tussman?" I asked Cassie. "Oh, I can't stand him, he's awful!" she exclaimed, not knowing she was addressing his son. She shared the common critique: he was authoritarian, unhip, uncool. I can imagine her argument now: "I don't need to read dusty old tomes by dead white men to be a good citizen! I have an innate feeling about what's fair and right and just and that's enough for me." "Oh, Cassie," my father might reply, "You've inherited a civilization that's been passed down and refined generation to generation for hundreds, if not thousands, of years. How can you critique it if you don't understand its foundations? Like Lear's daughter Cordelia and all the misguided flower children of the world you're ready to toss it all aside because you have a *feeling!*"

With this revelation I liked her even less. That evening we decided to drive down to Santa Cruz where we walked on the pier at sunset. Putting his arm around Cassie, Paul asked if she would spend the night with him. She consented so that night the top bunk was to have an extra occupant.

The next morning, I started the day by dropping a little acid. Paul and Cassie were going to walk across campus to the college and convinced me to accompany them. Arriving at the converted fraternity that was the home of the program, they decided it would be fun if I said hello to my father. Paul opened the door to his office and they pushed me inside. My father was seated at his large wooden desk. He seemed to fill the office as he rose to greet me. A student would later be quoted in *Time* magazine effusing that "his moral sense is almost physical—his presence overcame our skepticism about great men really existing."

I had no doubt my father was a great man. He was strong, athletic, powerful, like a Greek God, the antithesis of the image of the effete college professor. I believed he could be anything—an army general, a mafia don, president of the United States. He strode across campus like a Colossus. I remember passing him once in Sproul Plaza, feeling small and insignificant, despite my six-foot-one frame, as he failed to even notice me. His concern was not with the petty details of his academic career. His interest was in ideas—ideas that had lasted for thousands of years and would last for thousands more. The latest trendy sunglass-wearing continental philosophers whose objective was to deconstruct everything he held dear were of no interest to him.

"Are you okay, Davey?" he inquired, as I stood helpless trying desperately to look normal. I mumbled some reassurances and left as quickly as possible, heading down the street to the brown shingle house by the Seven Palms grocery where Ben lived a mere block away. Ben was seated, as usual, in his throne-like chair just inside the door. In front of him was a tray piled with white powder that he was coaxing delicately into gelatin capsules, samples of his latest score. I made up some reason for my appearance and we chatted a bit, Ben waxing philosophically, "Freedom is really just financial independence!" Those were not the words of a great man; they were the words of a seducer. As an idea, it was a wrong idea, but I was seduced. In that moment I felt like some precious secret had been revealed to me, a secret that made me special, that elevated me above all those poor students down on the UC campus slaving joylessly towards a dull and plodding future. I now knew for certain I was on the right path. In that magical white powder lay the key to my transformation and salvation.

B
en would sell me small amounts of LSD in powder form which l would put in capsules and sell to my existing clientele, or to anyone else who happened to knock on the door. My apartment became a hangout, various characters showing up at all hours. One of my best customers was a cultured blind gentleman named Bob who worked at the Berkeley Rep Theater. The "click, click, click" of his cane would alert me to his arrival. Bob always had something up his sleeve: he knew where he could score a hundred kilos of pot, he had access to ET, the base chemical for making LSD, but of course nothing ever panned out.

Gradually more and more friends, acquaintances and strangers would show up seeking to score or just hang out. l felt a little like Harold Fine in the hilarious Peter Sellers comedy *I Love You Alice B. Toklas* who gives up his strait-laced life for a hippie existence, whose brother shows up at his apartment- turned-hippie pad and exclaims, "What a groovy, groovy scene!" Leaning against the railing of the walkway outside my apartment, l felt a rapturous inner glow of satisfaction, thinking l was finally doing "my thing." What l was doing was certainly not my parents' thing, or anything else that had been expected of me, and it was intoxicating.

But it was all too good to be true. One day l got a call.

"Hi, this is Ed."

Ed, Ed, I thought. Didn't ring a bell, but I must know an Ed, or someone I know must know an Ed, I thought absent-mindedly.

"Can I come up and get a few hits of acid?" he asked.

"Of course," I replied. Ed appeared and I was surprised by his straight appearance, but he reassured me by saying he was from South Carolina. After the sale I walked him out to his car, obviously an unmarked police car, but I was in denial. Hopefully he would go away and I wouldn't see him again, but he came back and wanted more. Finally it dawned on me that Ed was Ed the Nark.

"Uh oh, I sold to a nark," I went around telling people, as if nothing was going to change. Such was my level of denial that I quit my job at the post office, thinking I no longer needed the income. But one night there was a knock at the door, and I peered through the curtain to see a badge staring me in the face. I grabbed the box that held my stash and tried to lock myself in the bathroom, thinking I would flush everything. A friend tried to push his way into the bathroom with me, for what purpose I can't imagine, and in so doing prevented me from getting the door closed. Before I knew it the police knocked down the front door, barged in, gathered us all up, and drove us down to the Berkeley City Jail.

They put me in a small cell with Alex, who paced about nervously.

"Let's rap!" he cried. I didn't want to rap. What was there to say? We were in jail, that's all. Soon we would be released, it would all work itself out. When offered my one phone call, I decided to call Mary Jane, a casual friend from the dorms who I hung out with occasionally.

"Hi Mary Jane, what's up?" I casually inquired.

"Not much," she replied, "What about you?"

"Well, I'm here in jail. I guess I sold to a nark."

My attitude of detachment recalls that of the character in Camus's *The Stranger* who reacts in a similar dispassionate way to his arrest for murder. I hadn't wanted to upset my parents by calling them. But unexpectedly and without being asked, Mary Jane called them.

"Your son's been busted," she announced to my father. I'm told that the news brought tears to his eyes. The next day the Berkeley *Gazette* grandiosely proclaimed the arrest of a "major campus supplier." After spending the night in jail we appeared before the judge, represented by a lawyer friend of my father. Charges were read, bail was set, and we were released back into a world that would never be the same for us.

Hours before my arrest my mother had penned a letter to her mother:

> It isn't a good day for writing. I feel very upset. Everyone seems to be. And yet I suppose they will slip back into their lethargy soon.
>
> I am busy writing an article on Henry Adams (the grandson of John Quincy Adams and descendent of the famous John Adams). I find him the most interesting American writer (he was an historian). But it's hard to write a short enough article. He was so complex...Well, I actually have written a book, the one Braziller wanted to publish—and that I have never really finished. It is not the way I want to write. However, that is the way I see the world. Reality for me is like rising to a surface and finding it transparent but impossible to break through—therefore what I see is always from below looking up to a world I can never enter.
>
> Today I'm sending you my thesis. I told you that New

York University wrote me about it—wanting to publish it—but I never did anything about it. Well, I hope now to get busy finishing a lot of things. I always felt unsure that I should. Anyway, a copy of my thesis is here in the library and is read often. I will send you the commentary about it. I guess I never did. Since the paper is thin, try to read it against a heavy plain background (I was offered a job at London University on the basis of it—with a research group on parliamentarism). I'm still interested in the problems and I did a lot of research.

Yes, I will send you copies of my articles—I have planned so many—goodness knows how I'll ever get them all written—and, of course, it takes a little time to write them in other languages...

That evening, on June 5, 1968, Robert F. Kennedy was assassinated in Los Angeles.

To my surprise, after my arrest, my parents, the lawyer they had hired, and others in their circle did not see my endeavors as exciting or heroic, but rather as the sordid indicia of a young life gone astray. I had to give up my apartment and move back with my parents. They were once again living together, although not really reconciled. My father had a new lover (having split up with Julia), one of a series he would continue to enjoy for the rest of his life, much to the distress of my mother who years later would write to him:

> I'm grateful to have had one great love affair. It was easy for you to go from one woman to another and I remember that you derided me because I am not like that. I am sorry that I was such a difficult woman for you. But I feel a little better knowing that those other women did not bring out the best in you. I wonder if the Joe who

"thought" (?) he loved me was "the real Joe." The young girl who loved you was the real Lorrie. Life defeats most of us.

I too felt defeated by life. What could the future possibly have to offer?

I had one tablet of LSD left, a blue wedge of something, so I decided to drive down to Santa Barbara to get away from it all and reflect. We had spent many summers in Santa Barbara, that beautiful oasis with its Spanish architecture nestled between the Santa Ynez mountains and the ocean ninety minutes north of Los Angeles. During summers my father had been a resident fellow at the Center for the Study of Democratic Institutions, a think tank of sorts started by Robert Hutchins, former head of the University of Chicago, in a beautiful mansion high in the hills above the town. Funded by the Ford Foundation, there some of the country's leading intellects would gather each morning around a long wooden table debating the crucial issues of the day as chosen by Hutchins. In the afternoons my father would join us on the beach, soaking up the sun, which was then considered a healthy thing to do.

I rented a room at the blue-roofed Miramar Motel in Montecito, in the neighborhood where we used to spend those lazy summers, took the blue wedge and headed to Joe's on State Street for dinner. Sitting at the counter I felt the acid starting to come on before I could finish my steak and spaghetti. In a panic I realized the dose was stronger than expected and that I had to make it back to my room as quickly as possible. It took all my will to focus on the task of driving back to the motel, but somehow I made it.

It is difficult to describe the agony of that night. Unable to walk or even stand, my brain felt as if it had shattered like

glass into a million sharp painful shards that would stab me
from within if I tried to move. My nervous system was short
circuiting in rapid fire flashes, like a gross magnification of
my normal self-consciousness. That self-consciousness,
always so paralyzing, had now become literally paralyzing as
in each flash I was both observing the world and observing
myself observing it in an ever-repeating recursive nightmare.
Surroundings were dissolving and swirling, there was nothing to hold on to.

When at long last the trip was over, spent from the
night's agonies I looked out the bathroom window. It was
dawn, the sun's light was soft and liquid and flickered off
the leaves of the trees. I looked down into the parking lot of
the All Saints by the Sea Church where the Sunday service
was about to begin. The minister was talking intently to two
beautiful young girls, doubtless his daughters, who looked
up at him attentively, a picture of human warmth and connection which I had never experienced, and doubted I ever
would.

Driving back to Berkeley, whatever reflection I had engaged
in on my short trip led me only in one direction. I realized I
had blown it, but all was not lost. I had a priceless connection for LSD. I had four or five regular customers, dealers
themselves, to whom I could sell virtually as much as I could
get. If I just abandoned my previous flamboyant lifestyle and
focused on a low-key middleman operation, I could continue
dealing with little chance of getting caught again. So, I went
to see Ben, who welcomed me back, correctly judging that
I was not going to set him up for a bust in exchange for a
reduced sentence.

Berkeley, and the Bay area generally, was becoming a hub
of LSD production and distribution for the country. Demand
and production were exploding. I was in the right place at the

right time, but I still had to complete my obligations to the legal system.

I had been caught "red-handed," so my only hope was to present a sympathetic case to the judge in hopes of a lenient sentence. Letters were solicited, including one from my old girlfriend's mother lamenting my unfortunate parental situation. I was presented as an impressionable youth who had been led astray by the drug subculture but had learned the error of my ways. The judge, noting skeptically that he felt everyone had been a bit taken in, nonetheless handed down a minimal sentence of ten weekends in the county jail followed by three years' probation.

One condition of the sentence was that I seek therapy for the course of my probation. My therapist was a tall, bearded gentleman who I didn't particularly take to. He talked a lot about "expectations" and my problems dealing with them, but all that talk seemed rather tedious to me. Once he called to change an appointment and my mother answered the phone.

"Is David there?" he had innocently asked.

"Who is this?" my mother demanded, probably thinking he was one of my drug connections. He refused to identify himself and my mother became irate, hanging up on him and complaining to my lawyer about his attitude.

As part of my rehabilitation, I was signed up for group therapy. Indescribable terror gripped me as I walked up to the colonial style house on The Alameda for the first meeting of our group. I sat quietly as each of the five other participants shared their stories with the two group leaders. None of them were of any interest to me, except perhaps one attractive young girl named Bridget. She was pretty and charming, but the others were another story. One of them, a chubby, ruddy faced redhead, was pushed to express his true feelings about his mother.

"Fat pig!" he exclaimed.

"Keep going," he was encouraged.

"Fat pig! Fat pig!" he cried with growing conviction.

Once when waiting for group to begin one of the members decided to confront me, bravely declaring, "Your problem is you just don't care about any of us, do you!"

I was shocked, "Oh no, of course I care," I stammered. She might have been right, but I didn't want to admit it. In any case, I was too fearful to share anything of my inner world. Secretly I felt that if they would just focus all their attention on me some incredible breakthrough might occur, and I would be healed. But I was not about to initiate that and of course it never happened.

After a couple of months, I could no longer withhold the secret from my therapist that I had resumed dealing. It was just too compelling a secret, one that made me feel special and alive. This could have been a big problem had the court or my probation officer chosen to inquire as to my progress in therapy. My therapist expressed concern about this but said that, in light of the circumstances, he could no longer see me, and I would have to drop out of the group. On my last visit he gave me a hug as I left, which I endured standing limply in the doorway.

Fortunately, my probation officer was very laid back. I would visit him every six months, we would exchange brief pleasantries, and I would go on my way. Meanwhile, I spent my required ten weekends in jail at Santa Rita, showing up Saturday morning and leaving Sunday afternoon, all of which proved very uneventful.

My arrest did have one very beneficial result. I walked into the Berkeley Selective Service office and asked innocently, "What is your policy regarding convicted felons who are currently on probation?"

"Well," the woman in charge stammered, "We probably wouldn't want you."

Sure enough, soon thereafter 1 received notice that 1 had been reclassified for purposes of the draft as category 1Y, meaning 1 was available to serve only in the event of a national emergency. Fortunately, the Vietnam War never rose to that level.

Business was taking off. Ben started selling me crystal grams of pure LSD, showing me how to buff it out into powder using endless cases of DCP which I would purchase at the Hub Pharmacy in San Francisco. Of course, only drug dealers would show up late at night to buy cases of DCP, but they didn't seem to mind. Each crystal gram contained four thousand doses. Adding a small amount of DCP to the crystal I would first grind it up with a large mortar and pestle, gradually adding more DCP, then transferring the mixture to a large glass jar, adding more DCP and shaking it up until properly mixed in the right proportion. Finally, I would weigh it out into bags of a hundred, five hundred, or a thousand doses. While doing this a fine powder would get into the air and into my lungs, meaning much of the time I was stoned to one degree or another. All of this took place in an apartment I rented as a "stash pad."

My new prosperity was beginning to show. I moved out of my parents' house and rented a brand-new studio apartment in a house on Panoramic Hill above Memorial Stadium with a stunning view of the entire Bay Area. I purchased a beautiful burgundy Porsche that I saw at the local dealer and could not resist. I took Julia (she and I remained friends after her breakup with my father) for a ride, declaring the car to represent the Platonic ideal of what a car should be. I would drop a little acid and thrill to the whine of the air-cooled rear engine redlining as I navigated the twists and turns of Highway 17 over the Santa Cruz mountains to Carmel, driving back home after a dinner of abalone on the Monterey pier. To my father I explained that I had succeeded in collecting some debts I was owed before my arrest, an unlikely story that he chose to believe as it was more palatable than the alternative explanation.

So, what was the life of a drug dealer like? In my case, not that exciting, really. Mostly it involved a lot of waiting—waiting for a drop from the lab. Then Ben would give me a call, "Meet me at the Plane of Time," and I would head over to the stairs which descend from the broad plaza at the Pacific School of Religion where we would affect the transfer. I would buff out the acid at my stash pad and deliver it to my waiting customers. No money would change hands, as the goods were always fronted. Money would trickle up from below in the form of small bills which I would change into hundreds with the help of a friendly teller at the Bank of America. I would deliver the proceeds to Ben, less my share, then wait for the entire process to repeat itself.

On a normal day I would sleep late, sometimes till noon. If it wasn't too late, I wandered down for breakfast, usually steak and eggs at The Brick Hut or the International House of Pancakes on Telegraph. Sometimes Price or our mutual friend Roy would join me. The three of us had formed a loose association, Price having followed me down the path of dealing. Then I'd usually head over to Dwinelle Plaza where several other fellow dealers hung out into the afternoon. Many of them kept drugs hidden in the student lockers at nearby Wheeler Hall. Or I would make rounds, visiting customers and sometimes hanging out with them. In the evenings there were sea food dinners at the Grotto in Jack

London Square, family style French meals at Le Petit Village on Shattuck, steak and lobster at Larry Blake's Anchor or Solomon Grundy's on the Berkeley waterfront. For pizza it was Giovannis, for Mexican it was the funky Mexicali Rose near the Oakland jail. For a special treat it was the exotic Khyber Pass in Oakland, which claimed to be the first Afghan restaurant in the U.S., or Hank Rubin's Pot Luck on San Pablo. Hank also owned Cruchon's, known for its fabulous fudge brownie pie. Sometimes for dinner we would be joined by Bill and his stunning girlfriend, Celeste. Celeste wanted to marry Bill, but he resisted heroically. Invariably I would return home alone to watch late night television, ending with reruns of *The Untouchables* on Channel 2, after which the station signed off by playing "Pachelbel's Canon" to soothing images of a beautiful mountain stream.

But there were also moments to be remembered. During the summer of '69 Ben announced he was getting married. We all headed up to Ben's country house outside of Healdsburg in Sonoma County. Situated on a couple of acres, a creek ran along the edge of the property where, upon my arrival, I found Juan leading a philosophical discussion. Probably everyone was on acid. "When I was at Yale, we were told to read *Man's Fate* by Andre Malraux," he began. "I refused to read it because Man does not have a fate!" A helicopter roared overhead. Was it the narks? No, it was the KGO helicopter rented by fellow dealer Curt who flew over the house dropping dozens of roses.

Curtis Blaine Rutherford was a true believer. Formerly in the military, he tried LSD and decided it would save the world—but only if it was *really pure* LSD. He once showed up at the office of Berkeley's underground newspaper, the *Barb*, which printed an article voicing his complaints about the proliferation of dealers selling inferior product. One evening when I was enjoying a slice of fudge brownie pie at Cruchon's, he walked in shaking his head. Art Linkletter's daughter had reportedly committed suicide by jumping out of a window, which her father claimed was the result of a bad acid trip. "If I had hair like that, piled on top of my head in a plastic bouffant, I'd jump out of a window too!" he asserted with a remarkable lack of empathy.

Ben's wedding ceremony took place in the driveway led by some sort of guru wearing only a loose gown with no underwear. He read from an ancient Vedic text describing the roles of the man and wife. Juan started heckling the guru, objecting to the sexist views. "Can it, Juan!" the bride's mother barked. Juan shut up, concealing a sheepish look as the guru droned on.

During 1969 the market for LSD continued to explode, and prices tumbled. While I had paid four thousand dollars for my first gram of LSD, by the end of '69 the price had dropped to two hundred and fifty dollars per gram. My goals had been modest; at first I thought that stashing away twenty thousand in addition to my Porsche would be fabulous, but I blew by that goal and by the end of 1969 I had accumulated one hundred thousand in cash, at that time a quite substantial sum. I stood on the balcony of my studio looking out at the twinkling lights. I had come a long way from my humble beginnings in the apartment on Channing Way. "I'm rich!" I declared to my friend Darrell, a former high school classmate from Connecticut who liked me better when I was poor.

New Year's Day, 1970. The decade of the '60s had finally come to an end. I recall no great celebration. Alone in my apartment the phone rang. "Hi Tank, what's up?" It was the voice of Celeste, addressing me by the nickname I had acquired due to my expanding girth. Her boyfriend Bill had departed, purchasing a TWA round the world ticket. His first

stop was to be India, accompanied by the well-known Bay
Area artist Michael Bowen who was going to help him pur-
chase Indian cultural artifacts and smuggle them back to the
US. Celeste couldn't stand Michael Bowen; he was too full of
himself. She didn't like people who thought they were groovy.
So Bill had left her behind in their tiny studio apartment on
Le Conte Avenue. She was all alone and had no money and no
job, but she did have my phone number.

Celeste's looks caused everyone to stop and take notice.
Tall, lithe and doe-like, with a quiet, deep, sensual presence,
she reminded me of my mother, but without the intellectual
dimension. Like my mother, she seemed wounded, fragile, as
if you needed to step lightly in her presence. I had considered
her completely unattainable, yet here she was, on the other
end of the line, desiring my company. I went and picked her
up, she spent the night, we made love. Her body next to mine
felt like the body of a real woman, I thought. The next morning, we went out for breakfast at the funky diner Buddy's Café
at the foot of University Avenue. I felt alive, expansive, full of
love for the world and everything in it. From that point forward, we spent every night together. She would arrive by taxi,
run upstairs, and I would give her cash to pay the driver. For
dinner we'd have steak and lobster, grilled on the hibachi on
my deck, followed by a quart of Dryer's Rocky Road ice cream.
Then we'd watch *The Untouchables,* the Pachebel signoff, and
drift off to sleep.

Celeste must have found me odd, but not entirely in a bad
way. Glancing in my closet, she fell to her knees in laughter
upon discovering that my wardrobe consisted primarily of
five pairs of identical brown corduroy pants I had purchased
at Bluebeards on Telegraph. I would pair these with a tur-
tleneck top, usually gold colored. Clothes had always been
a problem for me. Everything seemed uncomfortable and

ill-fitting. If I found something I liked I would wear nothing but that one thing, or multiple copies of it. When we lived in Connecticut my mother would take me to G. Fox department store in Hartford where I would marvel at the neatly folded rows of Arrow shirts. They seemed to represent a life of ease and elegance, one that I so desperately wanted to inhabit but seemed so unattainable.

Me with my mother and her sister in 1969

But to Celeste the most disconcerting thing about me was not my clothing, but my silence. She first noticed this driving up to my apartment one day when I seemed to run out of things to say. "You're being very quiet," she commented. How to explain that? I had no answer because I accepted the conventional wisdom that constant babbling was the desired norm. Small talk was not my forte. Neither was deep conversation. This would become a continuing point of contention.

She would point out how her friend Pat's husband was a volcano of emotions which were constantly erupting, whereas
my mind was like a steel trap, nothing ever escaped.

Somehow, we got through it all, but it was not meant to
be forever. Before Bill had left on his around the world jaunt,
he and Celeste had agreed that after he finished his business
plundering the cultural heritage of India they would meet at
the halfway point, on the Greek island of Mykonos. It was
decided that Celeste and I would do a brief European tour,
at the end of which I would see her off to Mykonos for her
reunion with Bill.

Meanwhile, the LSD business was becoming dangerous.
It was no longer just the local narks that one had to worry
about; the federal Bureau of Narcotics and Dangerous Drugs
was getting involved using new and more sophisticated tech-
niques such as wiretaps and conspiracy indictments. Had I
been arrested a second time the treatment would not have
been so lenient. Plus, my father was finally beginning to suspect what was going on. Then there was the problem with
Price.

Price's friend Vardan had also been lured into the drug
trade. Seeking to raise money to buy his salmon boat, he
headed to Amsterdam with a supply of LSD fronted to him by
Price. It wasn't long before his local competition turned him
in. Hearing this, Price immediately flew to Amsterdam, heading straight for the office of the magistrate handling the case.
"My name is Price Stiffler, I'd like to see my friend Vardan," he
announced.

"Oh yes, Mr. Stiffler," the magistrate responded. "We know
all about you." Vardan, it turns out, had spilled the beans,
describing in detail his LSD connection in the math department at UC Berkeley. Upon hearing this news, we picked
from the Bay Area stable of dope lawyers one by the name of

Morley Shapiro to see what he could do.

Morley was a charming and charismatic figure, a former NCAA diving champion who now worked for the firm of Hallinan, Hallinan and Hallinan. Vincent Hallinan, the father, was a legal giant, known for his defense of Harry Bridges of the Longshoreman's Union and many other radical causes; his sons were somewhat less impressive. Morley was just one of a coterie of attorneys who gravitated to defending drug dealers. The money was good and the lifestyle glamorous. So glamorous that many of them became a little too attracted to it. Morley was destined to be one of those, but at this stage of his career he radiated youthful vigor and enthusiasm. He gathered letters attesting to Price's character from his professors at Cal, travelled to Ohio where he had been an undergraduate and did the same, then headed to Amsterdam where he recruited a leading criminologist to assist in Price's defense. All of this probably had marginal effect, as both Price and Vardan ended up spending the next two years together in prison.

The final factor that led to my decision to retire was the fact that I now had a real girlfriend. So one day I marched off to my father's office, described to him in detail what I'd been up to for the past year and a half, concluding with the happy news that I was retiring. He listened thoughtfully throughout, not saying much of anything, no doubt pleased that I was quitting. What could he say, really?

It seemed like the right decision at the time. I had a hundred thousand in cash, which seemed like a lot of money. I turned over all my connections to Jim, who had been my best customer, and he went on to make hundreds of thousands more. I asked nothing in return. Had I been smart, I might have turned over all my other customers to Jim, kept Ben to myself and used Jim as a middleman. It would have been foolproof. But Tim Scully himself would years later tell me that l had made the right decision. Ben's operation had been busted and he was headed to prison, and many others in the trade were headed to equally unhappy endings. My part in the LSD saga of the 1960s may have been a small one, but at least l had escaped unscathed.

CELESTE

April 1970. Celeste and I flew over to London on the newly operational 747 jumbo jet. We had no specific plans other than that in two weeks we would separate and she would head to Mykonos to meet Bill. This was my first overseas trip, but I scorned the idea of planning and guidebooks, having the misguided idea that travel should be spontaneous. We landed in London at night with no accommodations booked. After a prolonged wait an agency at the airport was able to locate a place for us in a modest rooming house.

London was cold and drizzly, and we wandered about aimlessly. I learned that Scotland Yard had a crime museum which we attempted to visit. "No, you can't go in," the guard at the door said. "If we let people in it might give them ideas," he explained.

One day I set off to wander about on my own. I wanted to find the place in Hyde Park where people gave political speeches, but instead was accosted by a student from Algeria who asked me where he could find a metro station. I didn't know, but he didn't care. He traveled with rock bands giving them massages, he said, inviting me to his apartment. Why not, I thought. We had sex and I went back to Celeste after grabbing a burger at Wimpy's. I found it to be surprisingly good.

Having had enough of London, we took a hydrofoil across

the channel to France. The ride felt like we were inside a violent washing machine. We wound up in Paris trudging up the Boulevard St. Germain lugging our suitcases not knowing where we were going. "Keep on trucking!" Celeste would exclaim. We found a mediocre hotel and slogged through the Louvre and the Luxembourg Gardens, eating mediocre food and getting bored. So we decided to jet off to Nice. In the airport we spotted Rex Harrison, but Nice was more of the same, a mediocre hotel and mediocre food and nothing to do. I tried to visit a casino on the waterfront but was stopped at the elevator by the bouncer. "Pas comme ça!" he said. Clearly I did not have the appearance of a high roller.

Rome was next. We arrived at the train station and headed in the wrong direction, away from everything important, towards the Piazza Vittorio Emanuele where we found a room. In those days, a market filled the square seemingly run by gypsies. From our window I could watch chickens being slaughtered. We attempted to explore, always on foot, making it by accident as far as the Coliseum and once all the way to the edge of Villa Borghese Park. But we never saw the Spanish Steps, the Trevi Fountain, the Pantheon, Via del Corso, the River Tiber, or any of the other sights that tourists frequent. Near our lodging there was a theatre where we watched *Planet of the Apes* in Italian, and on the edge of the Piazza was a small trattoria where we had some of the best Italian food I've ever eaten.

After a few days our time together was over, so I delivered Celeste to the airport where she boarded an Olympic Airways flight to Athens. Feeling lost, I stood there in the airport lounge for several hours watching flights take off.

My European grand tour was not turning out as I imagined. Leaving Rome, I took a train to Geneva. I hated Geneva, so I boarded a long overnight train to Copenhagen. I shared a compartment with an American soldier on leave who said he couldn't wait for the pleasures of Copenhagen. Arriving at the train station, I walked across the street to Tivoli Gardens where I won a jackpot at some casino game I didn't recognize. I didn't know what to do with my winnings, so I kept playing until it was gone. Copenhagen was nice but I couldn't find any pleasures there, so after a few days I'd had enough and bought a ticket home on Scandinavian Airlines.

Imagining I was going to spend several months in Europe, I'd given up my beautiful place on Panoramic Hill, so upon my return I found myself in Celeste's tiny studio on Le Conte. Having nothing to do and no purpose in life, I devoted myself to obsessing about Celeste. There was only one telephone on Mykonos, which I would call almost daily in the unlikely hope that she might be nearby. Doubtless she was considering her options: stay with Bill, who still seemed implacably opposed to marriage, or go back to me. She chose me.

Her return to Berkeley coincided with the waning of my obsession. I went to pick her up at the airport in a gold Cadillac a friend had left with me thinking that would turn her off, but it didn't. I was beginning to realize that no longer was I to live in my world, from now on I was to live in Celeste's world, cramped in her tiny apartment, feeling the weight of her expectations.

We drove over to Bolinas to visit Michael Bowen. He was what my mother would describe as a live wire, talking nonstop and doting over the new baby girl he had named Ramakrishna, while I sat in silence. But there was no doubt, she had given up on Bill and now focused her desires on me. I knew I was not exactly her ideal of the masculine male. She bought me a sleeveless t-shirt, something like Marlon Brando might wear, but I just looked ridiculous in it. She met a studly Iowa farm boy who was her sexual fantasy and disappeared

with him for a night, confessing upon her return that he had
been too good to pass up. I gave her a lecture that probably
my father could have given about how she should think long-
term instead of pursuing momentary gratification. It was the
longest lecture I had ever given, to which she listened with a
bemused smile.

I had no clear idea what to do with my money, other than
a vague instinct that real estate might be a good investment.
My father suggested I go see his uncle Harry, who had made
a modest fortune in Marin County real estate. Harry called
and said dramatically, "Go to a pay phone and call me back."
I arranged to see him in his office where he mentioned that
there was still property in Marin County that you could buy
that would someday make you very wealthy. I leaned forward
in my chair eager to hear his next words: "But I think you
should buy a bookstore." A bookstore! How dreary! I mumbled some words of agreement and that was the last I talked
to Harry.

I did buy a couple of modest properties in Mendocino
County, but then, tired of the tiny apartment, decided to buy
a house in Berkeley. It was a little like trying to score my first
kilo. I looked at many but liked none. There was one I did like,
a beautifully remodeled Tudor style home on Regal Road. The
realtor was not too helpful. "I don't think you've quite earned
that house yet," she pronounced. True, it was listed at a pricey
forty-two thousand, so ultimately I settled for a house I didn't
like, a Cape Code style colonial on Grizzly Peak Boulevard for
a more reasonable thirty-six thousand. High up in the hills,
fog would roll through the Golden Gate and head straight for
us. Celeste decided that all the floors, beams, and trim should
be stripped and stained to expose the natural wood, something not exactly in character with a Cape Code house. But
nonetheless I spent months and months stripping, sanding,

staining, stripping, sanding, and staining. I'm sure there's still dust lodged in my lungs from that unhappy experience. We furnished the house in what might be described as hippie chic featuring Oriental carpets, rich velvet drapes, a large redwood burl coffee table, and big comfy pillows. Dealer friends such as Chris and John would come over for steak and lobster dinners in the backyard.

As far as my future was concerned, amazingly they decided to give me a third chance at UC Berkeley. I only needed a few more units to graduate and my plan was to then go to law school. It seemed like a reasonable path for a former drug dealer. "Somehow I can't really picture you as an advocate," fellow dealer Bert remarked perceptively when told the news. Celeste had a different view, imagining me in a three-piece suit with one of those watches attached to a chain that you kept in your pocket. I had observed enough lawyers at work to doubt whether I could do what they did, orchestrating a show of legal pyrotechnics. I knew I was very bad at thinking on my feet. But I couldn't think of anything else to do.

Prior to our trip to Europe, we had spent a few days on Maui and fallen in love with that magical island. Surprisingly, I had never heard of the place; to me Hawaii had meant Oahu and nothing more. So in May of '71 we returned for a full month, renting a condo on the shore at Honokowai, just north of the Kaanapali resort. Sometimes before sunset I would walk alone down the beach towards Kaanapali, the islands of Lanai and Molokai visible across the channel, in the other direction pineapple fields climbing the slopes of the West Maui mountains. Floating in the water observing it all by the fading afternoon light I felt a timeless sense of well-being. Celeste and I would drive down the coast past Kihei where you could find a spectacular beach all to yourself, or head around the east side to Hana where we went skinny dipping in the Seven Sacred Pools. The slopes of Mt. Haleakala with the quaint towns of Makawao, Olinda, Kula, seemed like paradise on Earth. Lahaina had the air of a lazy south seas port where we would grill our own steaks at the Pioneer Inn, or head down to Olowalu to Chez Paul which served the best French food I had ever tasted. We made friends with a local realtor named Virginia, who tried her best to sell us property, but we were in no hurry. Mistakenly, we thought time, and everything else, was on our side.

Swimming in the Seven Sacred Pools in 1971

August 3, 1971. Elvis Presley was to perform at the Sahara Tahoe casino in Lake Tahoe. A friend of Celeste's, a devoted Elvis fan, was unable to go and gave us her tickets. On the way up, Celeste's frustrations spilled over and things degenerated into an ongoing argument. Eventually neither of us could take it anymore. Celeste decided that the only way for us to make up was to surrender to the inevitable and get married. My resistance worn down, I relented. We rented a motel at South Shore and headed down into Nevada to the county seat of Minden where we obtained a marriage license and a gift package of household items to help us get off to a good start.

The County Clerk directed us back up to Lake Tahoe to the Justice of the Peace in Zephyr Cove. He called in two deputies to act as witnesses and there in front of his house overlooking the lake we were married.

Standing in the driveway after the ceremony we were both uplifted, swept away, transported into an altered state. It was what I had heard psychologists refer to as a peak experience. In the words of Maslow, we were experiencing "wonder, awe, reverence, humility, surrender, and even worship before the greatness of the experience." All of this we felt, together, in this moment of rapture and euphoria.

And then off to see Elvis. Not a big Elvis fan myself, I was surprisingly impressed. His performance was kind of a playful parody of himself. He was having a good time and so were we. It was before he had slid too far in his fight with the demons that would soon lead to his death.

Later I would call my father, casually informing him of the news. "Well, good luck, Davey," was his cool response. Celeste was a puzzlement to him. Having no intellectual dimension to her personality, they had nothing in common, nothing to talk about. I think the rawness of her emotion kind of scared him. It definitely scared me. Writing to my mother in Buenos Aires to give her the news, she replied,

I received your letter telling me about David. It was quite a shock. I guess mothers always feel that way. In my dreams he always appears as just a little boy. What can I say? Life goes on in its own way. One has control over nothing—even oneself. I wrote them a letter to wish them happiness. I guess I was glad to learn that she likes flowers and is good to plants. And I guess you all agree that she can't be a worse wife than I. I hope they are happy.

For our honeymoon we went on a six-week road trip through the western United States, starting with a relaxing week at the Mar Monte Hotel on East Beach in Santa Barbara. We went swimming, rode horses, played tennis, and made friends with the hotel manager who, dubiously, claimed she had once dated Elvis. Then on to Ojai for a night at the luxurious Ojai Valley Inn where we made love on the golf course.

Me with my mother and
grandmother Malka

The next stop was Santa Monica where we visited my grandmother, Malka. A well-known Yiddish poet, she must have been disappointed that I was the second generation of her offspring not to marry a nice Jewish girl. Nonetheless, my father had been her favorite son, and I was her favorite grandson, a fact that her other son, Hugh, never quite got over. He would often repeat the story that when my father was off at college, Malka would rob his piggy bank and send my father the money, admonishing him that "Joe mustn't know!" In typical fashion she showered us with love and attention. As a young boy when we would visit her house in Hollywood, her greatest delight had been to give me a bath. I would sit naked in the tub wishing I could disappear as she gazed lovingly at me repeating, "Mein kindt! Mein kindt!" It caused me such stress that the night before I would wet the bed in anticipation of the ordeal to come. But there was no doubt Malka was a remarkable woman. She was born and raised on a farm in the Ukraine with a couple hundred serfs that her father rented, Jews being unable to own property. One day Malka overheard some of them discussing how they were going to divide up the spoils when the pogrom came. Reporting this to her father, the decision was made to come to America.

After a day in Santa Monica, it was off to San Diego where we spent a week in a lovely condo on the La Jolla Cove, then a quick stop in Arizona to peer into the Grand Canyon and a night in Santa Fe, New Mexico. Next up was Colorado Springs where we stayed at the Broadmoor, an old-world hotel where, when checking out, they refused payment, saying instead they would send me a bill.

We drove through the entire state of Wyoming without stopping or talking at a hundred and twenty miles per hour, heading to Salt Lake City, then to Tahoe where we stayed in a condo on North Shore looking out over the lake, spending time watching the Oakland A's win the World Series. After a week there it was time to return home where Celeste gave me a tearful hug, sad that our beautiful honeymoon was over, but happy to have such memories to relive.

But there was a cloud of doom hanging over us, and her name was Cara. She was a freshman at Cal when I first met her in Deke's apartment behind the Top Dog back in 1968. She flirted with me and we had sex in Deke's living room. She claimed I was her first lover, but like so many of her pronouncements, I was not quite convinced it was the truth. She was from San Leandro, a small city just south of Berkeley, where her parents were dedicated members of the local John Birch Society. Their newsletter had featured an article, complete with picture, about my father, implicating him as an agent of the Communist Conspiracy on campus. To her credit, Cara did not believe in such nonsense. She was instead under the influence of *Cosmopolitan* magazine, which purveyed the idea that all was fair in love and war, and that trickery was the way to get a man.

Nothing was to come of our first encounter, but every so often we would run into each other. She knew that Celeste and I had married, but doubtless regarded this as only a minor inconvenience. While Celeste and I were spending a second month on Maui in May of 1972, Cara sent me letters which she knew would speak to the part of me that was neglected by Celeste. That part was my "awareness." I was potentially one of the most aware people she knew, she claimed, with emphasis on the word "potentially." Cara claimed to be a "witch," a woman of power. What that meant I wasn't quite sure, but it seemed to indicate that she might have the power to "fix" what was wrong with me, to help me overcome all that stood in the way of my happiness.

Berkeley in those years was a hotbed of what Cara referred to as "spiritual shucking and jiving." Groups like Werner Erhard's EST, Scientology, the Fisher-Hoffman process (which promised you a divorce from mom and dad), Claudio Naranjo's Seekers After Truth, various Eastern gurus and others offered to free you of not just your parents but of all the obstacles, self-imposed and otherwise, that prevented you from achieving freedom, self-actualization, and enlightenment. I had mixed feelings about these groups. Part of me was intrigued, but I also feared the self-exposure that the processes offered by them entailed.

Celeste was not intrigued. Once we went to see the movie *Rainbow Bridge* about a Jimi Hendrix concert staged on Maui by the Brotherhood of Eternal Love—the so-called Hippie Mafia. There is a scene where a young girl, seemingly interested in having sex with a member of the Brotherhood, is lectured by him about the spiritual virtues of abstinence. "Just fuck her!" Celeste yelled at the screen, as my friend Darrell and I slumped in our seats hoping not to be noticed.

October 28, 1972. Tina Turner was to perform at the Berkeley Greek Theatre. The same friend who had given us the Elvis tickets invited Celeste to go. It was perhaps inevitable that instead of staying home alone I headed straight for Cara's apartment where we made love for the first time in four years. In Cara's arms it felt like all the pain and sorrow I had kept inside all my life was released in a flood of emotion and tears, emotion that it would not have felt safe to reveal to Celeste. But Cara, woman of power, knew just how to evoke and guide and manipulate that emotion. It went on for months. Several times a week, instead of going to class, I would show up at her door, drawn to her like a moth to flame.

Eventually the madness took full hold of me. I believed that my future life, my very existence, depended on leaving Celeste and being with Cara. The hard part was leaving Celeste. I agonized endlessly, dreading that moment when I would have to reveal to her the news, in all its stark cruelty. Finally, one day, the words just came out, "I don't want to be married anymore." Celeste looked stunned, incredulous. In one moment, her life had been upended. Why, and for what? Rejecting her for Cara? That could only have been the ultimate insult. And so I left that evening, went to a pay phone, and called Cara.

"I did it, I left Celeste!" I proudly announced. Cara too seemed stunned.

"Well, come on over then," was the reply. I drove over to her humble one-bedroom apartment off Telegraph Avenue in Oakland, which was now to be my new home.

This was not a peak experience. There was no sense of shared euphoria, ecstasy, transcendence. It felt uncomfortable, unnatural, like a great effort that in some strained calculus was someday going to pay off but of course never did. From the moment I moved in I was unhappy, and it only became worse. I was not "fixed" but in fact regressed to an almost infantile state as an escape from the horrific consequences of what I'd done. Cara continued her spiritual shucking and jiving, of which I now wanted no part. She went on her own to a Seekers After Truth event where Claudio butchered a lamb in his bathtub, then took everyone to see the movie *El Topo*. I joined them for the movie, remembering only scenes of horsemen riding through a dark landscape littered with animal carcasses. "Oh, the symbolism, the symbolism!" Cara would mutter in awe.

Celeste herself descended into a despondent state, at times stalking us, taking a knife to our yellow sofa, haranguing me relentlessly. Once she cleverly applied paint to Cara's license plate, which read "CRAFTY," changing it to read "CRAPPY." I liked that. She kept living in our house, trying to digest what had happened, trying to figure out how to repair her life.

Cara and I went on a road trip to Canada and had a miserable time.

Then came the period of flip-flopping, as Cara would call it. After the unhappy trip, something inspired me to reconnect with Celeste. We went away for a weekend to Santa Barbara. It was a wonderful time. I realized that there had been a richness, a texture, a beauty to our life together. With

Cara there was nothing, but she was not about to tolerate any more flip-flopping. One day, realizing I was up at the house with Celeste, she drove up, parked, and stomped inside. She went directly to Celeste, grabbed her by the hair, and dragged her across the living room screaming "He's mine now!" Then she turned to me. "Get in the car, David!" she commanded.

For a moment I hesitated and considered my options.

"No, David, don't do it. Don't go. Come back," Celeste softly pleaded.

"Why not?" I thought. Wouldn't that just put an end to all the confusion and heartache? Or maybe I should just wash my hands of both and face life bravely on my own. No matter, it was over in an instant. Cara pushed open the door and I meekly walked out and got in the car. Something told me I had to go, there was still some unfinished business I had with Cara on which my life depended.

But I was not completely ready to let go of Celeste. Sensing that, Cara would insist that I call her and tell her that she and I were finished. "Make the phone call or leave!" she would demand, relentlessly. I refused to make the call, and I refused to leave.

Things then progressed to the next stage: marriage. For Cara it was a fairness issue. I had married Celeste; therefore, I should marry Cara. Surely she deserved equal treatment. Cara took on the project by herself and arranged everything. Resistance was futile.

Finally, the wedding day came. Standing in front of the mirror of our bedroom putting on the uncomfortable blue suit we had bought for the occasion, I went through the motions of preparation like a zombie, on autopilot. There would be the ceremony at the church Cara had found in Alameda, a wedding buffet at the Alameda Naval Air station. Then we would drive down to Carmel, rent a random motel room for the night for a perfunctory honeymoon that we would terminate early. Everyone was already on their way to the church. I considered for a delicious moment not showing up. No, that would attract too much attention. But in the back of my mind I knew, somehow, someday, I would make my escape. It might take a while, it might take years, but that day would come.

A PROMISING YOUNG LAWYER

I started law school in 1972. I wasn't sure I wanted to be a lawyer but couldn't think of anything better to do. My father encouraged me, as he would like to have been a Supreme Court justice, but that was hardly my destiny. While I counted the weeks until graduation, still three years away, my classmates gradually transformed themselves into baby lawyers, showing up in three-piece suits indicating they had gotten jobs working as clerks in firms with long impressive names. A world of plodding conventionality, punctuality, and dependability that I certainly was not made for. As to what I would do when I graduated I hadn't a clue, but probably my mind was on other things. I would deal with the future when it arrived.

I left Celeste during my first year of law school and married Cara in my second. My grades were passable, but I decided that for my third and final year I would make amends. The secret to success was simple: attend every lecture and take copious notes. I took very good notes, got the highest grade in two of my classes, and finished the year in the top five percent. But it turned out that was not the secret to success in finding a job. I discovered too late that if you did not already have multiple offers well before graduation you were considered a failure and unemployable. And those offers were based on your record in the first two years and on the contacts you made clerking and interviewing during that time, none of which I did.

Not totally discouraged, I spent the summer of '75 studying for the bar exam, which I passed easily, and sending out a few resumes, none of which generated much excitement. I did get one interview with a small firm in San Diego. We drove all the way down from Berkeley with great optimism. "You won't be on the market much longer!" Cara exclaimed. I put on the same suit I had worn to our wedding and set out from our Travelodge motel for the interview, feeling a bit of panic as if I was going to get married again. The lawyer who interviewed me was nice enough. His hobby was flying airplanes, and I pretended to be interested. I also pretended to like San Diego, and to want a career with a good firm where I could someday become a partner. Then he sprang the question: "Do people take you seriously?" he asked, "or do they sometimes look at you and think you must just be kidding?" A little nonplussed, I had to admit that I sometimes had that problem.

Eventually I landed a job working for a lawyer in downtown San Francisco. He hired me because I could type, and the job required a lot of typing. My first project was to prepare over a hundred complaints. This was before the days of computers so instead he had stacks of forms for the various situations that arose: car hits car, car hits pedestrian, car hits house. I had to review the file, select the right form and fill in the blanks. His clients were insurance companies who hoped he could recover for them a portion of what they paid out in claims. This was called "subrogation," an obscure specialty that had never even been mentioned in law school.

When I first showed up for work, I was impressed with the appearance of efficiency and prosperity. There was an office manager, a receptionist/secretary, a bookkeeper, and a part time "default clerk" who spent all her time taking defaults of defendants who didn't bother to file a response when sued (most of them didn't). But a few weeks after starting I came in one day to find he had fired everyone but me.

My employer was not a terribly brilliant lawyer but had learned to bluster his way through and win by persistence—the American way. After I finished filing the hundred complaints, I started drafting pleadings and making court appearances. I enjoyed the challenge of untangling the intricacies of civil procedure but was well-aware that subrogation was the lowest rung on the litigation ladder. I was making five dollars an hour with no prospect for advancement. Fantasizing that if I had my own clients I could charge much more, I had cards and letterhead printed, but of course I had no clients. Then one day, alone in the office with the radio on, I heard an interview with Byrd Baker, an anti-whaling activist, talking about the upcoming Greenpeace campaign to save the whales. Moved by the thought of these people who, rather than spending their time filling in the blanks in subrogation complaints, were venturing onto the high seas in Zodiac boats to confront the whaler's harpoon, I called and left a message volunteering my services.

Up to that point the decade of the 70s had seemed a bit depressing after the excitement of the 1960s, which I had spent pursuing the glittering temptations of the Berkeley counterculture. But the youthful energy and idealism unleashed in the 60s quickly dissipated, replaced by the general spiritual malaise of the 1970s. It seemed there were no great causes or movements left to capture my fancy. Besides, I was married and supposedly trying, half-heartedly, to construct a middle-class existence.

But there was one bright spot: a colorful mixture of traditional peace activists and idealistic counterculture characters from Vancouver who had gotten together to start an environmental movement called Greenpeace. Sparked by opposition to U.S. nuclear testing in Alaska, their first endeavor was to sail a small boat into the test zone near Amchitka Island as a protest in the nonviolent Quaker tradition. The boat never made it and the tests were cancelled, but soon the scene shifted to the South Pacific where the French were conducting their own nuclear tests at Moruroa. David McTaggart, a former builder and promoter of ski resorts from Vancouver whose hand seemed to have played out in that field and had left it all behind for a life sailing the high seas, happened to be in the area and responded to an ad placed by Greenpeace looking for volunteers to stage a protest. The French were none too pleased and during his second voyage into the test zone in 1973 commandos boarded his boat and beat him severely. McTaggart moved to France to pursue a lawsuit against the French government and began sowing the seeds of a Greenpeace organization in Europe.

After the French tests were cancelled new causes emerged: the killing of whales by the Soviet fleet in the Pacific and the annual slaughter of harp seals on the ice floes off Newfoundland. In the summer of 1975 Greenpeace attracted worldwide attention when a Soviet ship fired a harpoon over the heads of its protestors who were in a small Zodiac boat trying vainly to protect a sperm whale from its pursuers. Bob Hunter, Greenpeace's spiritual leader and media strategist, believed this would be the searing image—the media "mind bomb," he called it—that planted in the world's consciousness would lead to a fundamental change of attitude towards the environment. His ideas of social change were borrowed from Isaac Asimov's work of psycho-historical fiction, *The Foundation Trilogy,* and in honor thereof Greenpeace became the Greenpeace Foundation, a legal entity incorporated under the British Columbia Societies Act. When groups of supporters began to organize in far-flung places, they couldn't have been more pleased. The tribe would expand, and the newcomers would channel their enthusiasm into raising money that would funnel up to the tribal elders in Vancouver to support the ever-expanding Greenpeace agenda.

To encourage their growth in the fertile United States, Hunter and his wife Bobbi visited the newly opened San Francisco office in the spring of 1976. One item on their agenda was to incorporate Greenpeace in this country and apply for tax-exempt status, and for that a lawyer was needed. Going through the messages left at the San Francisco office on Second Street in the trendy but still inexpensive south-of-Market area, Bobbi spotted one from a lawyer. The name—Tussman—sounded vaguely familiar. One of the elders from Vancouver, Rod Marining, had spent his senior year at Simon Fraser University studying the writings of an obscure American political philosopher from Berkeley named Joseph Tussman, my father. His first book, *Obligation and the Body Politic*, discussed the role of the citizen in a democracy. Tussman argued that our political system had been corrupted by the competitive model of the marketplace. Citizens in a democracy, being in fact the ultimate authority, had a higher obligation than to use the political process to pursue their own selfish ends, or the ends of some group or constituency of which they happened to be a member. One should base political decisions not on what is best for one's private interests, but what is best for the community. Such ideas were not terribly popular with students at Berkeley—they were cynical about the political process and were only interested in how it could be manipulated to achieve revolutionary change. But my father's idealism did appeal to a tribal consciousness where wise elders would get together, deliberate, and arrive at solutions. Rod had described these ideas to the elders, who agreed they suggested the correct governing principle for a voluntary organization such as Greenpeace.

With all this in mind—or perhaps not—Bobbi picked up the phone and gave me a call inviting me over to the San Francisco office to discuss how I could help. I was thrilled. Bobbi turned out to be a simple, shy, quiet girl who spoke in the endearing Canadian accent, soon to become so familiar, in which most sentences end in "eh?". She introduced me to the others in the office, local Greenpeace supporters who I would work with in her absence. Bobbi went back to Vancouver and I enthusiastically set about incorporating the group with the ambitious name Greenpeace Foundation of America. Three of the local members served as the incorporators: Marion Yasinitsky, the motherly office czar, Al "Jet" Johnson, a dashing American Airlines pilot with Robert Redford looks, and Gary Zimmerman.

Gary was president of the local group. He couldn't have cared less about tribal rituals, honoring elders, or the obligations of a tribal member. He was an engineer who just wanted to use his expertise to go out and save whales. Along the way he would organize Greenpeace in America and raise money to support the effort. He was an American and this was a democracy, not a tribe. So what if the Vancouver group could articulate with such eloquence the apocalyptic neo-Luddite vision, then common among environmentalists, that technology-dependent western civilization was about to collapse, leaving it to the Greenpeace navy to sail the seas protecting the planet from greed and destruction? It seemed like the Vancouver bunch was busier talking than saving whales. Results—the body count of whales saved— were what mattered, and while Vancouver talked whales were busy being killed! There were plenty who sympathized with those views, including a renegade faction in Vancouver led by Paul Watson. Paul had developed a more radical activist philosophy that he called—without a trace of irony—"aggressive nonviolence." Soon to be expelled from Greenpeace for his provocative actions during a protest of the harp seal hunt, he started his own organization and would travel the world sinking whaling ships, getting things done, and speaking out against the do-nothing Greenpeacers who he seemed to loathe as viscerally as the whale killers themselves.

Shortly after we became acquainted Gary began paying regular visits to my office on Montgomery Street. He thought he had a mandate from the Vancouver founders to make the San Francisco office into an autonomous umbrella organization for Greenpeace in the United States (by this time, independent groups were springing up in places such as Seattle, Portland, Eugene, Los Angeles, Santa Cruz, San Diego, Boston, and Hawaii). But now, he complained, Vancouver was trying to sabotage and undermine his efforts. I was not aware of the substantiation for his grandiose claim of authority, and certainly the other U.S. groups were none too thrilled about it. Innocently, it had been my suggestion that it would be easier if the U.S. legal entity were structured as an independent group so that in applying for tax-exempt status it would not appear that it was controlled by a foreign organization. I had not foreseen the need to draft documents recognizing in Vancouver some form of ultimate control over the use of the Greenpeace name—it was all just one big family, or so I thought. That oversight would have fateful consequences for the future of Greenpeace.

I listened patiently to Gary, musing that all this was just normal internal politics for a group filled with people with abnormal egos.

On one occasion Gary wondered out loud, "What side are you on?" I wasn't on any side, since I liked everybody. When

the Greenpeace ship *James Bay* docked in San Francisco in
July 1976 on its way out for the second annual anti-whaling mission, 1 was awestruck. This was the most inspiring
group of people 1 had ever met. They were on a life-or-death
mission to save the whales and ultimately the planet, and
they radiated camaraderie, humor, and love. There was Bob
Hunter, gaunt and intense with an electric intelligence and
wit, ready to lose his sanity on a moment's notice; Pat Moore,
the PhD ecologist, pudgy and professorial, much the opposite of Hunter; Paul Spong, the passionate whale researcher
whose love for his subjects seemed almost physical. There
were only occasional signs of dissension. At a meeting on the
boat Paul Watson, wearing a Palestinian headdress in protest
of the Israeli raid on Entebbe, refused to sign a release for
the making of a movie based on the Greenpeace story. Bob
Hunter had earlier sold the rights to an outfit from New York
called AEC (Artist's Entertainment Complex) after meeting
in a bar with its agent, Amy Ephron. Amy had flown out from
New York to meet the ship to get everyone to sign releases,
driving up in a limousine wearing a short black dress with a
gaping round hole in the back, an apparition from another
world. For the next couple of years Greenpeace would be
a colossal pain in her neck, and the movie would never be
made.

There were also people 1 liked in the San Francisco office.
One of them was Cindy Baker. She had been hired by Gary
Zimmerman for the position of "Regional Coordinator."
Originally from the Greenpeace Portland office, her job was
now to tell the Oregon Greenpeacers, and everyone else in the
U.S., that they were branch offices of Greenpeace Foundation
of America headquartered in San Francisco. Her former
friends in Oregon wanted nothing to do with that. During
the spring of '77, when Greenpeace was between campaigns,

we became friends, going out for frozen yogurt (or Jack Daniels, her favorite drink) to discuss her frustrations with Greenpeace politics. Cindy didn't take kindly to frustration. She was on a mission, made more urgent by the fact that, only in her mid-twenties, she was dying of cancer. She had just completed chemotherapy treatments and now dedicated every ounce of her considerable energy to Greenpeace. I had a crush on Cindy, but Cindy wasn't interested in me because she was interested in Gary Zimmerman. That, however, inspired a way for me to demonstrate my devotion.

A group of Greenpeace supporters, helped by Vancouver, had organized in Hawaii and purchased a former U.S. Navy sub chaser renamed the *Ohana Kai* that they were outfitting for their own voyage to save the whales. Gary was in Hawaii to help them and hadn't seen Cindy in some time. I dreamt up the idea of treating Cindy to a trip to Hawaii. She would get to experience the beauty of the islands, check up on the progress of the *Ohana Kai*, and not incidentally have a brief reunion with Gary. I also invited Carole Sears, a volunteer in the San Francisco office, to tag along.

We flew to Honolulu sipping free champagne on Western Airlines and checked into a suite high on the twenty-fourth floor of the Sheraton Waikiki. Gary came over and we stood on the balcony marveling at the spectacular view of Diamond Head. He had been working nonstop on the *Ohana Kai* for days without bathing, and it showed. "Gary Zimmerman, I'm going to have to report you to the sanitation department!" Cindy exclaimed, as they departed to attend a Greenpeace Hawaii meeting. Carole and I stayed behind and strolled around the beach watching the glorious sunset.

The next day we paid a visit to the *Ohana Kai,* then in the final stages of preparation for its voyage to confront the Russian whaling fleet. Hard at work on the deck I spotted a young blonde girl in overalls who looked up and smiled at me; at least, so I imagined. Her name was Debbie Jayne, I would later learn.

The four of us flew over to Maui, rented a car, and drove down the long winding road to Hana. We rented a suite at the Hana Kai Hotel where Cindy enjoyed a night alone with Gary. I could hear them laughing in the bedroom next door as I lay listening to the crashing surf from Hana Bay outside the window.

On our return to San Francisco Cindy, who had taken over running the San Francisco office, decided it was time to add me to the Board of Directors, probably because she thought I would go along with her wishes and vote to get rid of her nemesis, Bob Taunt, also known by his full name of Robert O. Taunt, III. Taunt was a newcomer to Greenpeace who offered to organize a benefit concert but rapidly got involved in substantive campaigns. He was smart, confident, eloquent, outgoing, and ambitious—but perceived by many as pompous, elitist, and harboring suspect motives. Beneath that ebullient exterior lurked a hint of tragedy. He had worked in the California state legislature, had a healthy interest in politics, and had devoted a good deal of energy to opposing the Vietnam War. He also had a taste for the finer things in life, something which I found appealing but might have offended some elements in Greenpeace. He claimed his family owned a Lear Jet, but the promised rides never materialized. When he joined the voyage of the *James Bay*, he showed up with several trunks filled with clothes and expensive camera gear.

At my first board meeting Marion Yasinitsky presented a motion thanking Bob for his media work on the spring seal campaign but ejecting him from the board. Bob was flabbergasted. Everyone seemed in favor of the motion, but no one could articulate a good reason. One couldn't just say that he was a little too elitist or that people didn't like his arrogance and ambition, or that he just didn't fit the Greenpeace image with his trunks filled with Nikons and Hasselblads. Or that he had made the mistake after a few too many Jack Daniels of confiding to Cindy that he was soon going to be president of Greenpeace Foundation of America. Cindy, of course, was perfectly happy with the current president. I failed to speak up in his defense. Perhaps I hadn't found my voice yet, or perhaps I didn't want to betray Cindy. The motion carried.

Besides being someone Cindy could depend on, my main project was to apply for tax-exempt status so Greenpeace could qualify to receive tax-deductible contributions. After much back and forth with the IRS, it was eventually granted.

Meanwhile, a plan I had nursed for some time was becoming a reality. To jump-start my legal career, I applied to the graduate program in tax law at New York University. Although the fall semester was still several months away, I resigned my subrogation job, stating that I was leaving "to pursue other interests"—I had heard that expression somewhere before and always hoped I would have a chance to use it myself. For the moment my "other interest" was to spend the summer volunteering full-time for Greenpeace.

Soon the *Ohana Kai* would venture out on the first anti-whaling voyage not organized and run by Vancouver. They found the Soviet fleet, but there were no whales around. A small party of Greenpeacers decided to board the huge factory ship, driving their Zodiac up the slipway where the whales were hauled to be butchered. They distributed buttons and leaflets in Russian to the surprised crew. ABC Sports had paid to place a film crew and helicopter aboard the ship and produced a special that was shown as an episode of their *American Sportsman* series. After this brief encounter, the *Ohana Kai* limped back to San Francisco where it became the derelict waterfront home of assorted Greenpeacers, destined never to sail again.

That summer the *James Bay* also saw action, so for a time Greenpeace had two vessels patrolling the Pacific, the beginnings of its global navy. When the *James Bay* stopped for refueling in San Francisco a benefit concert was hastily arranged at Pier 33 where the ship was docked. Jerry Garcia with some of the Grateful Dead and the singer Maria Muldaur performed. It was a beautiful day and the *James Bay*, flags waving in the breeze, rocked dramatically back and forth behind the stage while the crowd enjoyed the music in the bright sunlight. It was a magical moment, highlighted by the fact that it marked the beginning of my brief fling with Judy, the new office manager who had just been hired by Cindy. Judy invited me over to her apartment where I wound up spending the night.

The next morning I dragged myself home to Berkeley where Cara awaited. I explained that I had drunk too much at the concert and fallen asleep on the *James Bay* where there were no telephones to call her. She probably didn't believe it but was unable to shake my story. It was but another reason for her to resent my involvement with Greenpeace. But she could understand the attraction. One evening I took her to Bob Taunt's where we passed the time drinking and playing darts with Bob and a couple of friends. We were having a splendid time. Cara turned to me and exclaimed, "No wonder you hang out here all the time, it's so much more fun than being at home!" Then, having had a bit too much to drink, she ran to the bathroom and threw up.

When September came Cara and I rented out our house in Berkeley, packed up some things, and flew off to New York for my year at NYU. But when I got in line to register every cell in my body cried out in revulsion—how could I have forgotten how much I hated school! I stuck it out for a week or so. We looked around half-heartedly for an apartment, finding that New York was a crumbling city in decay. New Yorkers couldn't have cared less about the environment or about saving whales. It was all they could do to survive another day. Eventually I got up the courage to go into the registrar's office and withdraw. I said I had been offered a job back home, and after consulting with my family had decided to take it. The dean was incensed—I had wasted one of the most coveted spots in any American graduate school. We rented a car, checked out of the Americana Hotel, drove up through Harlem and out of New York. After a brief tour of New England to see the autumn leaves, we flew back home.

My story about the job was not too far from the truth. Upon my return, Cindy put me on the Greenpeace payroll at the standard rate of eighty dollars per week. Since our house in Berkeley was rented out for the year, Cara and I had to find another place to live. I wanted to be in San Francisco, preferably in Pacific Heights where I could be close to the new Greenpeace office in Fort Mason. Cara, who until now had gone along with everything I did, almost put her foot down when she saw the awful green shag carpeting in the flat I located in an old Victorian on Octavia Street. Even on that she soon relented, but things were not auspicious for the future of our relationship. I had almost left several times but hadn't gotten up the courage. I had gotten to like Cara and there was no real reason we couldn't stay together, except for the fact that married life felt like a death sentence, and I needed to experience something new and exciting.

The end came on Halloween night in 1977. Upon returning from New York, I had reconnected with Judy. She had been invited to a Halloween party in Berkeley and invited me to tag along. That seemed new and exciting enough, so that day I told Cara I didn't want to be married anymore. Judy and I went to the party, but they were all young college kids who were about as uninterested in me as 1 was in them. 1 didn't talk to anyone.

After that Judy and 1 never really got serious. We went to bars after work at Greenpeace and drank Irish coffees, but that was about it. Cara soon moved out. After the breakup she commented wistfully, "Didn't you want to have a life like my parents?" 1 thought in horror of her father, wasting his entire life running the hardware store he had inherited, and her mother, an energetic suburban housewife who ran everything else. For now, 1 wanted to have fun, and Greenpeace, among other things, was a lot of fun.

Bob Hunter and Bob Taunt enjoying good times at Taunt's flat on Liberty Street

One person who seemed to know how to have fun was Bob Taunt. Although fired by the San Francisco office, the Vancouver group wasn't about to let him go. It was his connections, despite a number of cover stories, that provided Greenpeace with the coordinates of the Russian whaling fleets in the Pacific. He had Walter Cronkite's home phone number, was friends with California Governor Jerry Brown and Congressman Leo Ryan, and was about the only U.S. Greenpeacer that Vancouver felt was a real asset to the cause. Although officially he had little connection with the San Francisco office, his Liberty Street flat in the Noe Valley neighborhood became something of an alternative Greenpeace nerve center. Here, as wherever Greenpeacers gathered, there was much drinking, flirting, and mostly innocent good times. From my perspective, everyone involved seemed sincere, honest and well-intentioned—or was I just a bit innocent and naive?

A NOT SO PEACEFUL GREENPEACE

As fall of 1977 turned to winter, things began to change at the San Francisco Greenpeace office. Gary Zimmerman had had enough and faded away, eventually moving to France to marry a woman he had met on the *Ohana Kai*. Cindy Baker's body had had enough and she returned home to Oregon where she died a few weeks later. There was no longer a president of Greenpeace Foundation of America, nor was there anyone eager to fill the position. I moved into Cindy Baker's old office and became what I called, tentatively, the "Acting Executive Director." But in reality I didn't dare exert too much authority. There were too many people watching me suspiciously.

Feeling the need to clean up the organizational mess resulting from Greenpeace's undisciplined growth, Vancouver called a meeting and invited representatives from all the Greenpeace offices, large and small. It was held at the home of Bill Gannon in the Kitsilano neighborhood of Vancouver. Bill was an intense young accountant who had drafted the infamous ABC system of accounting which Vancouver sought to impose upon all Greenpeace offices, whereby a third of each group's income would be remitted to Vancouver.

As a result of the meeting a committee was formed to draft proposals for an international structure to be presented to a second meeting to be held in January 1978. Bob

Taunt was named chair. Other members included Margaret Tilbury from Oregon, Carlie Trueman and Bill Gannon from Vancouver, and me. Though we met half a dozen times, we had little idea of what a complex task we faced. Those who gathered in Vancouver in January were a wildly diverse group, consisting of factions within factions. San Francisco alone had three distinct groups. There were the elitist "executives" from the headquarters office at Building 240 Fort Mason, of which I was obviously a member. They counted the money

A group photo of the first International meeting in October 1977, with the Vancouver skyline in the background. I appear sixth from the right in the top row.
© Greenpeace / Rex Weyler

and controlled access to the telex machine. The "grassroots" element—called "the yahoos" by some—occupied a second building at Fort Mason. They included the foot soldiers who went out every day to raise money by selling merchandise or soliciting door-to-door donations. The third group consisted of those who lived and hung out on the *Ohana Kai*. They were the dreamers, an assortment of free-spirited Greenpeacers

from all over. The boat had become a minor tourist attraction and offered tours during the day and communal meals
at night. Even San Francisco's poet laureate, Lawrence
Ferlinghetti, showed up regularly.

When January rolled around, all the factions within the
Greenpeace universe in North America had representatives,
some accredited and some not, at the meeting. But glaringly
absent was anyone from Greenpeace groups outside of North
America. David McTaggart, leader of Greenpeace Europe,
which was only beginning to organize itself, appeared for
the first day but in what he called an "unofficial" capacity. He
made it clear that Europe was not ready or willing to participate in our process. "I don't want to step on anyone's little
knackers," he apologized in his typically polite but dismissive
manner. But we should organize North America first, he
insisted, before we presumed to organize the world.

Nonetheless, good feelings abounded as the meeting got
under way. Space had been rented at a conference center
on the grounds of the University of British Columbia. Two
tall totem poles stood guard outside. A camera crew from
the local media showed up the first day for interviews. Bob
Taunt took his place at the head of the gathering, seated
in folding chairs arranged in a rectangle. "My name is Bob
Taunt, and I'm from San Francisco," he began, with his usual
sense of drama. Over the next four days he gently prodded
the group towards accepting the creation of an international
Greenpeace entity to coordinate activities and impose a minimum of accountability. It was finally agreed to establish a
governing board consisting of seven representatives, each of
which had to receive the vote of two thirds of the delegates
and no more than two of which could be from any one office.
On the first ballot no one qualified, but on the second try I
was the first person to be elected.

Then things began to get difficult. Two members from Vancouver were elected, but one of them was John Frizell, leader of the rebel faction. With his hunched back, scraggly beard, nasal voice and disheveled appearance he was the antithesis of charisma. John wasn't a bad person. He just wanted to save the planet, but the other Vancouverites wouldn't let him; he wasn't from their tribe. With loathing they referred to him as Gollum after the subterranean villain from Lord of the Rings, a traitor that had grown like a cancer in the tribal body. His election meant that out of seven board members the tribe would really have only one representative, Patrick Moore. It didn't occur to the others, or even to me, that this would be a problem. Everyone was just naively voting for people they liked. Wasn't this a democracy? Wasn't Greenpeace a dream, and wasn't it impossible to own a dream? Shouldn't anyone who had the same dream have just as much a right to participate in it as anyone else? As the meeting got bogged down in trying to fill the last slot on the board various motions were floated to create an exception allowing Bob Hunter to have the final spot. They were all voted down. Frustrated by the stalemate and worn out after taking fifteen ballots, Taunt called a break late in the afternoon.

When everyone returned, Hunter walked into the room dressed in black and looking angry. Taunt sensed there was trouble. "I hope there are no alcoholic beverages in the room," he warned. Hunter stood up to deliver what he described as a point of information. "Eight years ago we started off trying to do this trip. A lot of us have worked very, very hard. I know, everybody says that—four months, five months, four years, whatever! Well, we just had a counterrevolution in our group against a power takeover that happened last year. And so now we have on our board no less than five people who have been involved in Greenpeace for eight years, and we have a very

David McTaggart, left, at the Vancouver meeting with Bill Gannon, Greenpeace Vancouver's financial guru

A break in the proceedings—from left to right, John Frizell, Michael Bailey, Liz Tilbury, Gary Young, Paul Spong, John Sargent, Bob Hunter (head bowed)

Bob Taunt presiding over the Vancouver meeting, January 1978

John Cormack, Greenpeace's father figure, captain of the first Greenpeace voyage to Amchitka

Paul Spong (left) and Dexter Cate (right)

Patrick Moore has a word with Carlie Truman as Nancy Jack listens in

well-worked-out relationship with each other and a very good group decision-making mechanism. Now, we were operating on the principle that this Greenpeace thing should be international. We were strongly in favor of calling this gathering. We hoped that the family would expand. We're opposed to the whole corporate power structure that's responsible for killing this earth! They're the ones who organize themselves according to power blocs instead of in any kind of organic tribal fashion. We were hoping we could transcend that level with this group. We acted on the advice of a poet named Allen Ginsburg who when we asked, 'How do you deal with power?' said, 'You let it go before it freezes in your hand.' Following that advice, Paul Spong went around, I went around, Bobbi went around, Pat Moore went around. A whole bunch of us went around and we kept saying 'Far out, start a Greenpeace group, let's go, let's move forward together.' And we gave away and we gave away and we bent over backwards to the point where now we are lying on our backs with our legs spread and all we see is people who have been here for one month, four months, whatever, rejecting us as being more experienced or in any position as elders. John Frizell got voted in because he appeals to the disaffected. Well, that's fine! The point of information comes down to this: that's it! We can't take it any longer. Our analysis is, the way this international meeting is going we will have lost any serious input into Greenpeace whatsoever. We have no choice but to withdraw. We are pulling out. Pat Moore, our president, wants to stay and talk to people, but the rest of us, we're fed up!"

Taunt listened with a dazed and bewildered look. "Mr. Hunter, you're out of order!" he declared. Cries of "Let him speak!" were heard as Taunt continued. "Now, I have as much respect for Bob Hunter as I have for myself, and that's a lot of respect! But this process has been democratic. I'm sorry if some people's sensibilities have been hurt, but we all feel that something has to be done to move Greenpeace towards an international emphasis. I don't want to see this organization run into the gutter any more than anyone else."

Hunter resumed. "Look we are trying to be responsible to a very heavy responsibility. I'm not going to accept, none of us are going to accept anything that lessens the seriousness with which we take that responsibility. The reality of the matter is, by the law of prior usage we own the name Greenpeace. We've been trying to give it away in a graceful fashion and instead we are finding people grabbing for too much of that power too soon on the basis of unilateral individual actions and parochial concerns. We all see the small games going on here, we all do! The decision of our board is irrevocable. We are leaving. You can talk to Pat, but the way this situation is going down, we just can't hack it!" Hunter and the rest of the Vancouver group got up and walked out, leaving Patrick Moore to reason with the infidels.

There were cries and sobs and sad speeches from those who remained. "What do you really want, Patrick?" Debbie Jayne demanded. Like most there, she saw the walkout as a bit of street theater designed to pressure the others into acceding to some petulant demand—more power politics. Patrick sat thoughtfully, then admitted he wasn't sure what they wanted. If he didn't know, then certainly no one else did.

One by one, the remaining delegates spoke. Throughout the four days I had remained quiet, speaking only when called upon by Taunt to give my thoughts on some point under debate. But when it came my turn, the room fell unusually silent. Partly it was curiosity, because I had spoken so little, but I believed, not entirely presumptuously, that most there liked and respected me and would value my opinion. I didn't know what to say, but I had to say something. "I've been involved in Greenpeace for over a year and a half," I began, unaware of the irony in that statement in light of Hunter's sarcastic remarks. "I became part of this committee because I hoped we could organize an international structure that would help Greenpeace be more effective. Vancouver has walked out because they didn't like the way things were going, but we shouldn't give in to pressure tactics. It is sad that it has come to this, but all we can do at this point is go back to our respective offices and continue our work for Greenpeace." Perhaps there could have been a way to salvage things, but it was late Sunday, everyone was tired and had plane reservations home, and as McTaggart had warned, Greenpeace was just not ready.

The meeting broke up and most of us returned to the Hotel Silvia, home to the out-of-town delegates, where chaos reigned. Hunter showed up and met with Taunt and me in a closet in our room. There was no talk of any solution.

"I remember," Hunter mused, "when I once took a workshop in Gestalt Therapy from Fritz Perls when he was living on Vancouver Island. He came up to me during a break and asked, 'How many of the people in this room are really going to get what this is all about?' 'Not very many,' I replied."

Taunt nodded in agreement. The rabble was swirling about outside, and in their ignorance the fragile dream of Greenpeace was being ripped apart. This was fate. Let something beautiful into the world and it would be defiled, not as much by its opponents as by those who believed but understood not. The yahoos would win out. No more would Greenpeace be guided by a tribal clan gathered in a circle consulting the *I Ching*. The center could no longer hold the energy that had been unleashed. Hunter's idealistic, utopian vision of a Greenpeace organized on a tribal model had been cast aside with little reflection. The tribe had been replaced by the mob.

When I returned to San Francisco with the rest of the delegation we were greeted as heroes for standing firm against the
Vancouver scoundrels—those "snakes in the grass," as some
called them. But I did come back with something positive
from all the turmoil. I had become enchanted with Debbie
Jayne, one of the three delegates from the Hawaii office known
collectively as Charlie's Angels, all being female, young and
beautiful. It became my obsession to reconnect with Debbie
at all costs, and the opportunity soon presented itself. Debbie
was organizing a fundraising walkathon in Hawaii scheduled
for the end of February, and I arranged to go as an unofficial
representative from the San Francisco office.

"The Angels"—Charlotte Funston, Nancy Jack, and Debbie
Jayne—on the beach at Waikiki

AN INTERLUDE

I flew to Honolulu, rented a car and drove to the Royal Hawaiian Hotel, the Pink Palace of the Pacific. I left the car in front and went up to my room in the tower building where everything was soft and pink. The trade winds blew gently through the curtains of the balcony looking out to Diamond Head. If there was ever a perfect moment of antici-pation this was it. The Angels had left a note at the front desk welcoming me. I called the Greenpeace office and they came over for a walk on the beach and a tropical drink at the bar. Then Debbie and I went up alone to the room. She was soft and pink with long blond hair and shy playful eyes. We made love on the pink sheets strewn with petals from my fragrant leis of tuberose and plumeria.

Debbie left to complete her preparations for the walk-athon, and I spent the evening alone in a state of excited anticipation. The next morning, feeling light as air, I ran the entire ten-kilometer walkathon route around Diamond Head. As reward for her hard work, the Angels had arranged for Debbie to have a few well-deserved days of vacation, and she was going to accompany me on a sojourn to Maui. Clearly the gods were on my side.

One minor obstacle had to be brushed aside. Shortly after my arrival at the Pink Palace I began to be peppered with phone calls from Bob Hunter. Vancouver had decided to make another effort to resolve the international situation and Hunter was going to San Francisco in a day or two to meet with people there. Not knowing what he was up against, he urged me to fly back immediately for the meeting. I resisted heroically, and as arranged Debbie and I flew off to Maui in a Royal Hawaiian Cessna.

Nancy Jack, one of the Angels, had loaned us the use of her tiny little cottage in Lahaina. No bigger than a large closet, she called it the shoebox. We went to dinner at nearby Kimo's on the water. Lahaina still had the feeling of a lazy south sea island port town, before it was to be totally ruined and overrun with tourists beginning in the 80s. When I first visited Maui in 1970 one felt part of a special elite for having discovered this secret paradise. Soon the secret would be out and visitors would traipse over in droves from the mainland to "do Maui." We sat looking over the water down the coast towards Kihei and Makena. It was a dark night and the stars twinkled above. I remembered sitting there several years earlier with Celeste watching the flashes from navy test bombing of the island of Kahoolawe. But for me the real fireworks were yet to come—that night in the shoebox alone with Debbie.

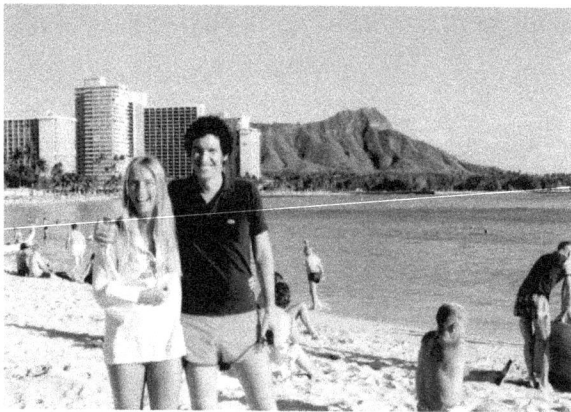

Debbie Jayne and me on Waikiki in 1978

"Oh Deb Jayne, I'm...just...so...crazy...about...you!" I said, struggling to find words to express the depth of my infatuation.

"It's not worth betting the farm on," she replied, sensibly. Debbie had a boyfriend who she lived with back on Oahu. I was not quite sure how she arranged to get away, but I was glad she did.

The next day we flew off to the Big Island of Hawaii, driving down the coast to Kilauea. We rented a cottage at Volcano House, a small hotel perched on the rim of the crater where you could sit and watch steam rising from below. I bought a couple of bottles of Liebfraumilch, the only wine selection available, and we retired for a final night of frolic. The next day we flew back to Honolulu, where I boarded a jet for San Francisco. I hugged Debbie frantically as we said goodbye, got on the plane, and sat there in tears. The tourists seated around me looked tan and rested and ready to go home. They had had nice vacations, but I had been to paradise.

"IT WAS REAL, SEAL"

Shortly after my return Bob Hunter made his promised visit to San Francisco. It was all for naught. He made a brave appearance before the assembled staff and volunteers to give a speech of reconciliation, but he seemed pained and ill at ease. He had poured his heart, soul, and genius into the Greenpeace cause, yet all he could generate that day were blank stares from people who, like ungrateful children, couldn't have cared less. After that he would slowly fade from involvement in Greenpeace, handing the baton to Patrick Moore. While Hunter, for all his faults, had been generally liked and admired—and worshipped by many—one could not say the same for Patrick. Patrick wanted to be liked, and I wanted to like him, but his overbearing manner sometimes made that difficult. Certainly he was not a very astute politician. Like Hunter, he must have been genuinely befuddled by the bloated entity calling itself Greenpeace that had taken root in San Francisco. While those who had given birth to the organization struggled to make ends meet in Vancouver, San Francisco seemed awash in money, but no one appeared to be in charge, and it had no agenda or environmental campaigns it could call its own.

Attention shifted to the spring campaign against the Newfoundland harp seal hunt. Vancouver was beset by financial and political woes, and by bitter memories of the

1977 seal campaign when Paul Watson had gone rogue and Brigitte Bardot had been on the ice, creating something of a circus atmosphere. They were more than happy to hand off responsibility for the 1978 campaign to Bob Taunt, who began its planning and execution from his nerve center on Liberty Street, with assistance from myself and others in the San Francisco office. Since Vancouver was unable to fund his efforts, Taunt asked if I could arrange a salary from the San Francisco office. Wanting to make amends for not standing up for him when he was purged the year before, I took the matter to the board. Bob had requested a thousand dollars a month, a princely sum to most Greenpeacers. To avoid making it an issue about Bob Taunt, I proposed that my salary also be raised to a thousand dollars and that Gary Young, Bob's friend who worked as financial director, be increased to eight hundred dollars. This caused an outcry and polarized the office like nothing before. I argued that we needed to pay more realistic salaries to attract the kind of people who would be needed as Greenpeace grew. The proposal was approved in a raucous meeting, after which Dexter Cate, one of the leaders of the yahoos, confronted me. "Do you want my take on all this?" he demanded. "The least dedicated people in this office are now being paid the most money!"

Dexter had a point. Of course he was more dedicated. He would work day and night for nothing if need be. And who was I anyway? Nobody had any idea what I was doing, or scheming, in my little office up in Building 240. I had demonstrated little interest in sailing out into the Pacific to risk life and limb to save whales or trudging out onto the Newfoundland ice floes to confront angry seal hunters wielding hakapiks. I hated boats. They made me seasick, and the idea of being in such cramped quarters with twenty or thirty other people was suffocating. As for the hakapiks, I was not really cut out

for confrontation and probably would have wound up apolo-
gizing to the hunters for bothering them. Why should I get a
thousand dollars a month in precious Greenpeace donations?

Truth be told, I had something of an aversion to the
extremely dedicated. They could be a little too sanctimonious
in their self-righteousness—or perhaps I just felt intimidated
in their presence. The Vancouverites were different. They
were dedicated, but they also believed that saving the planet
should be fun. They smoked, drank, and didn't worry about
their own purity or judge others by whether they were envi-
ronmentally correct in every detail.

Once Bob had his salary, things got into high gear. The
Canadian government launched a public relations campaign,
sending a delegation to tour the US giving press conferences
defending the hunt. Learning of this, Bob hustled off to New
York to organize a counter press conference which he held
at Essex House, and he began putting together a delegation including US Congressmen Leo Ryan and Jim Jeffords,
actress Pamela Sue Martin from television's *Dynasty* series
and assorted others to go to the ice to witness and protest the
hunt. The eccentric head of Oakland-based World Airways,
Ed Daly, had volunteered to transport the entire group to
Newfoundland in his private plane but backed out at the last
minute, possibly due to pressure from the Canadian government. We scrambled to buy commercial airline tickets for
everyone, all charged on my personal American Express card.

The grassroots element in San Francisco, working on a
parallel but separate track, had a different vision of how
the campaign should take shape. They had connected with
a Native American medicine man from southern California
named Grandfather Semu, who proposed to go to the ice and
conduct a fire stick ceremony on behalf of the seals. Taunt
and I met with his emissary, Sacheen Littlefeather, whose

claim to fame had been the fact that she had accepted Marlon Brando's Oscar for The Godfather on his behalf the year he had boycotted the ceremony. But Grandfather Semu didn't make it to Newfoundland; there were only so many seats on Daly's plane, and they had been promised to the aforementioned politicos and celebrities.

Ready to board their flight to Newfoundland to protest the seal hunt—from left to right, Steve Bowerman, Patrick Moore, Pamela Sue Martin, Bob Taunt, Monique van de Ven (a Dutch actress), Gary Young, Rex Weyler

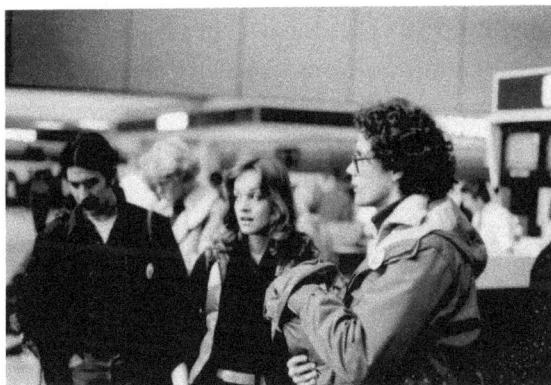

Rex Weyler, Bob Taunt and Pamela Sue Martin

In the end, the campaign was a mild success. A photograph of Patrick Moore squatting on the ice with a seal between his legs to protect it from hunters was flashed around the world—not exactly media mind bomb material.

"It was real, seal." My autographed photo of Patrick Moore sitting on a seal as Bob Taunt looks on in the background. As soon as Patrick was escorted away by the RCMP a waiting hunter clubbed this seal to death. © Greenpeace / Rex Weyler

After the campaign Taunt invited a small group on a vacation excursion to San Blas, Mexico, in a friend's private plane. Debbie Jayne came over from Hawaii to join us. We flew down the Pacific coast in the small plane, watching for cows on the landing strip at San Blas as we arrived just moments before dusk, after which it would have been too late for a landing. In San Blas we were taken under wing by an eccentric building contractor from New York named Norm Goldie who walked around with his pet parrots, caught fish for the hotel where we stayed, and was on the local boxing commission. But Debbie and I were not destined to recapture the magic of those nights at the Pink Palace, the shoebox and Volcano

House. From totally different backgrounds, we seemed to have very little in common. That was the end of my great romance. Debbie and I would reconnect for brief visits several times over the next few years, but the old passion was no more and we eventually lost track of each other.

Me and Debbie Jayne in Puerto Vallarta in 1978

A SORRY DAY

In 1978 Greenpeace continued in limbo and a kind of somber funk. An anti-whaling voyage was set in motion by a fly-by-night Greenpeace franchise in Los Angeles run by a group of Hollywood hangers-on turned environmentalists. Bob Taunt, Nancy Jack, and Patrick Moore were brought in as a troika to run the campaign using a vessel with the unlikely name M.V. Peacock, but it felt like a television sitcom that had run its course, and this was to be the last Greenpeace anti-whaling voyage in the Pacific.

That fall San Francisco Mayor and Greenpeace supporter George Moscone was murdered along with gay supervisor Harvey Milk. I got the news as I was sitting in my office being interviewed by FBI agents trying to track down a scheme to bomb whaling ships using a miniature yellow submarine that had been seized in Florida.

Then tragedy struck Bob Taunt. He had hinted to me with a touch of his usual grandiosity that he was on the verge of a major announcement that would result in his relocation to Washington, D.C. His friend, Congressman Leo Ryan, was on the House committee dealing with the environment and was going to appoint Bob as his advisor. I was driving to San Francisco for a gathering at Bob's flat to celebrate the happy news when I heard the announcement on KCBS: Ryan had been reported shot by members of the People's Temple in

Jonestown, Guyana, where he had gone to investigate claims of abuse by Jim Jones, leader of the Temple. What was to be a happy occasion turned into an all-night vigil as we waited for news to trickle in. Before leaving for Jonestown, Ryan had given Bob a phone number to the Situation Room in the White House, just in case anything happened. Bob called and spent much of the night getting reports from Zbigniew Brzezinksi, national security advisor to President Carter. Ryan was soon confirmed dead and his aide, Jackie Speier, who Bob had been dating, spent the night lying seriously wounded on the airport runway.

Bob Taunt was not destined to go to Washington. Instead, tired of the endless conflict in Greenpeace and shattered by the death of his friend, he gave up the public arena, got married, and retired to homes in Montana and Carmel. He was no longer Sebastian Flyte, I was no longer Charles Ryder, and the world had lost its charm.

The final blow came with the arrival in San Francisco of Peter Ballem, a lawyer from Vancouver, on May 11, 1979. A rugby player with a dominating physical presence, he was calm and deliberate but intensely serious as he sat at the conference table in the meeting room at Fort Mason stating the terms of his ultimatum to the San Francisco board. They must acknowledge that Vancouver was the legal owner of the Greenpeace name and sign an agreement, grandly called the Declaration and Charter, giving them limited autonomy under Vancouver's control. San Francisco lawyer Bart Lee, an informal advisor to the yahoo faction, responded. He was the opposite of Ballem, something of a poet and intellectual. Hugely overweight, he drove an MG Midget that tilted precariously under the strain of his bulk. Bart was there to defend the accidental entity known as Greenpeace Foundation of America. When advised that the San Francisco board refused to accede to his demands, Peter shook his head sadly. "It's a sorry day," he lamented.

The world had collapsed, and I was at its center. Within a few days Vancouver filed a trademark infringement suit—Greenpeace Foundation v. Tussman—seeking to prevent the San Francisco office from continuing to use the Greenpeace name. Their lawyers had advised that it would create an unfavorable impression if it appeared that Greenpeace was suing itself, so I was named as the primary defendant. The real story was obvious: Greenpeace was suing Greenpeace, but newspapers all over the country soon reported that Greenpeace was suing me, alleging that I had been hired to set up their branch office in the U.S. but had betrayed them, instead setting up a rival group that now pretended that it was Greenpeace. Pat Moore held a press conference at the San Francisco Press Club to announce that the local Greenpeace office was a renegade imposter that was soon to be brought to task; the renegades organized a counter press conference immediately following. I sat uncomfortably with the renegades in my dark suit trying not to look like a shifty lawyer, but feeling like one nonetheless.

It sounded serious, but I was not worried about my own fate. I knew they weren't after me personally. It was intriguing that I was a central figure in this drama and that my testimony was critical in determining the outcome. But I had no idea what I should do. There were pressures, and sympathies, on all sides. Pat Moore had been badgering me for a long time to take charge of the San Francisco office and deliver it back to its rightful owners. He thought I must secretly control everything since there appeared to be no one else of much substance. But his approach to persuasion was similar to a bull in a china shop.

On one occasion, Patrick stormed into my office at Fort

Mason, apparently thinking I just needed to be bludgeoned into submission. It was the culmination of what had not been a good visit for Patrick. He had arrived in San Francisco a couple of days earlier—it was August of 1978, just after the anti-whaling voyage of the *M.V. Peacock.* Patrick and I had gone out to the Balboa Cafe where he outlined his latest plan to resolve matters, which he would present to a board meeting the following day. After a couple of drinks, he became belligerent, promising to see to it that I was "ruined professionally" if I didn't vote to accept the proposal. The next day, a sober, calmer Patrick showed up at the home of Carole Sears in San Francisco's Sunset district where the meeting took place.

Patrick began on a conciliatory note: "Thank you for calling this meeting on such short notice—I would have allowed more time, but I have to return to Vancouver as I've been away on the Peacock for two and a half months. The first thing I'd like to say is that I am rescinding the letter of revocation signed by me on behalf of the Board of Directors of Greenpeace Foundation, and to further wipe the slate clean I withdraw my resignation as an ex-officio member of the San Francisco Board of Directors. I request approval of the Board for both of these."

Patrick was referring to his actions after his previous proposal to found an International Board of Trustees was rejected by the San Francisco board back in April.

Eddie Chavies moved to accept, and Falvey seconded, but then Dick Dillman jumped in with a bit of cautionary advice. "We should postpone this until after we have heard the whole proposal," he protested.

Flustered, Patrick pointed out that "meetings are held to reach decisions. If the Board doesn't wish to reach decisions..."

"We didn't mean that," Dillman clarified.

By now my head was spinning I knew this meeting was a

waste of time, and no one was going to agree to anything, but in my role as Secretary to the Board I continued taking copious notes.

Patrick attempted to move on. "We shouldn't get totally bonkered out on dope and booze as there are complex things to work out. To start, there are a number of points. Some are observations on where we stand, others require eventual resolution, others are prerequisite to continuing a coordinated, consolidated effort on behalf of Greenpeace. Certain areas have been neglected in the past due to political, personal and other obstacles. I've spoken to everyone here to some degree regarding certain aspects of what I'm thinking. I want it agreed that we drop the designation 'Greenpeace International' in favor of 'Greenpeace Foundation' or just 'Greenpeace.' We should keep capital lettered designations simple—no pomp and circumstance. There will be no such thing as an international or national headquarters. I don't know how we will get around this externally but for internal purposes our headquarters are in our heads. This will further the aim of decentralization. But we have to have an agreed upon plan—plans for campaigns so we have something real to do in the Greenpeace spirit."

Chavies jumped in. "I have a question regarding confrontation. A Newfoundland newspaper article quoted Pat as saying that Greenpeace was not trying to interfere with the seal hunt. I took offense at that!"

"Here is the explanation," Pat offered. "Of course, everything we do is attempting to interfere with the hunt. But our lawyers will argue that I was not interfering with the hunt under the law. That is, by sitting on a seal I was not doing anything illegal. Therefore, in a legal sense there was no interference."

Falvey sounded concerned. "I hope we are not committed

to not breaking the law. It is implicit in our ideology that we will occasionally break the law."

"The lawyers' approach is always to argue that we did not break the law," Patrick clarified. "If that doesn't work, then we bring up the argument of necessity—we did it to prevent a greater evil. The objective in this trial is to be acquitted. We want to establish a legal right to sit on seals—just like we have a legal right to get in front of harpoons. We aren't trying to water down the fact that we are trying to interfere with the hunt."

Patrick continued. "I had a lot of time with good lawyers in Newfoundland and here in the US—entertainment, corporate lawyers, Ed Bernstein, who is lawyer for Esalen, Joan Baez, grape pickers, with the movement for fifteen years. He is a man of incredible stature. I respect his opinions regarding what has to be done to create an organization that can grow and prosper, avoiding the pitfalls of other organizations. The basic question is this: are we one organization or are we a group of distinct, separate legal entities? Are we the same or two—San Francisco and Vancouver—that just happen to be cooperating? There must be a yes or no answer. Once you answer this, everything else falls into line. On the one hand, all of us accept that spiritually, financially, organizationally we are the same: Greenpeace. But we have reached the limits of growth under the present system. We need consolidation, centralization before we can get any bigger. We can't keep track of it all any longer."

"Are there specific people or contacts in mind or is this just a general concept," Falvey inquired.

Moore responded. "To be specific, Ed Bernstein said, 'Get your shit together kid, then come to me.' Or take the situation with rock stars. You can't have four different people approaching them, each claiming to represent Greenpeace. We need

somewhere to go where you can clear these things up. When
Vancouver visited San Francisco in 1975 with Zimmerman
and Jackson on the crew after the campaign, Vancouver was
forty-five thousand dollars in debt for the first time in history. We were in deep shit. The strategy was to establish an
office in San Francisco to protect the Greenpeace name and
create a financial center in the U.S. San Francisco was adept
at raising money—people were brought in who were capable
administrators."

Moore finally arrived at the moment of truth. "So a central
decision is required here. As far as what's required to consolidate, the San Francisco Board should resolve that Greenpeace
America recognizes that the legal right to the name
'Greenpeace' resides with the Greenpeace Foundation of 2108
West Fourth Avenue, Vancouver. In exchange, Greenpeace
Foundation shall guarantee the right of Greenpeace America
to operate with total autonomy regarding its own internal
organization and with total authority in Northern California.
We would also authorize an executive committee of initially
seven members, two of whom shall be members of your
board. Initially the committee will deal just with international campaigns, implementation of the financial system,
and the centralization of membership services. After a six-
month period of these seven working together—we want to
keep it simple, inexpensive, and practical at first—eventually
the group would have the confidence to develop a charter we
can all sign. But first we have to establish credibility. After six
months the committee can meet and decide whether or not
to add one person from Portland and one from Seattle, to further democratize the committee—hopefully as a springboard
towards Greenpeace Global. Conceptually, that's it I think.
It's an honest attempt at compromise and consolidation. I am
totally flexible regarding any honest ideas to improve this."

Silence followed. Finally, Carole Sears spoke up. "It looks like everybody is letting it sink in rather that opening their fat mouths for a change."

"There is a time for reaping and a time for sowing—expansion and consolidation," Moore continued. "We can't let growth happen again until we can consolidate. I see an army of ten fucking millions of people smashing fucking industrial states. Corn growing without insecticides. More birds again. We called Greenpeace a Foundation because of Asimov's Trilogy—where a group of people got together and recognized that the world was falling apart and through the science of psychohistory a dark age was predicted—ecological collapse. They set up a foundation and a second secret foundation at the other end of the galaxy. By changing consciousness, like getting in front of a harpoon—media mind bombs, Hunter calls them—they built a consciousness to shorten the time of the dark ages."

I listened to this rant with a bit of amusement. Smashing industrial states? Patrick did not seem to me like someone who would do that. If there was anything he wanted to smash it was the San Francisco office and anyone else who questioned his role as leader of Greenpeace.

"Who is The Mule?" Chavies asked, referring to a pivotal character in the Trilogy whose ability to manipulate human emotions enables him to become one of the great conquerors of all time, thereby threatening the work of the Foundation.

"It's nobody within us," Moore responded. "Let's make it easy and call Watson the mule. No, that's too easy."

"We do have a problem of a mule," Chavies pronounced. "There will be no decision this evening."

"I came here with a solid commitment not to get drunk beforehand and to remain calm," Moore pleaded. "I have a solid commitment to see that Greenpeace is really revolutionary. I walked into the University of British Columbia faculty club with Jerry Rubin and drank all their whiskey. I housed draft resisters and deserters. I'm from a radical background. I don't want creeping revisionism or liberalism in Greenpeace. We have to stay peacefully hard line. We can be a massive movement by being strong, peaceful, nonviolent but right on the fucking edge. This is not a threat—but I've found myself screaming and yelling at Greenpeacers worse than Newfies."

"We don't need an international for this," said Sears.

"No growth for growth's sake," said Chavies.

"Clear the decks of karma first," said Falvey.

According to the official minutes, the meeting flowed into incoherence.

Patrick's frustration was understandable the next day as he closed the door to my office behind him. From his perspective, the San Francisco board had been insolent, evasive, completely unwilling to grapple with the difficult issues facing Greenpeace. In the reception area outside my office concerned San Francisco staffers milled about anxiously. Carole Sears called Dick Dillman at his work and urged him to come right over. Dick was in charge of Greenpeace radio communications, and he was a good communicator. At an imposing six-foot-four-inches, he rode a Harley police special and didn't take nonsense from anyone, although his persuasiveness sprang more from his calm aura of moral authority than any physical intimidation.

Patrick demanded that I write him a check for ten thousand dollars to help pay his legal expenses in connection with the spring seal campaign. His act of sitting on a seal meant he was facing a possible jail sentence for allegedly "interfering" with the hunt. I couldn't do that, I protested. I called Gary Young, our financial manager, and he advised that we didn't have the funds (which was true—even though everyone thought we were rolling in money, in truth we always seemed just barely able to scrape by), and in any case such an expenditure was not within my sole authority. Cracking under the pressure, we wound up screaming at each other, just as Dick arrived to defuse matters.

Patrick's wife Eileen used a more subtle approach, more in the vein of seduction. "We'll have so much fun!" she once cajoled, inviting me to imagine us running around the world as the leaders of an elite corps of swashbuckling environmentalists, if only I would give in and wrest San Francisco's cash cow from the grip of the infidels who controlled it. The fact that I wouldn't was inexplicable to her, leading her to draw the only possible conclusion: "You're not really very smart after all, are you?" she asked, a bit provocatively.

Of course, those infidels in San Francisco, who I had to deal with every day, expected me to be on their side. After all, I was their lawyer, and they assumed I must loathe the snakes from Vancouver as much as they did. There were occasions when I was as guilty as anyone of pandering to the fear of Vancouver's draconian desire to control all of Greenpeace. But I didn't have the heart to reject either side outright, and I felt guilty for getting everyone into this mess—even if it was really that fool Allen Ginsburg's fault.

The honorable thing, in view of my conflicting loyalties and ambiguous role, would have been to step aside and allow others to determine the outcome, but that seemed too boring. Greenpeace needed to be delivered from the evil Gollum and the unwashed masses who threatened to usurp the organization in the name of democracy. The Vancouver elders had their faults but their dream had been stolen and I would return it. Acting in secret I would negotiate a settlement with Vancouver, giving them a majority on a joint governing board, and present it to San Francisco for approval. I knew I could deliver three votes out of seven on the San Francisco board, so all I needed would be one additional vote. Surely one poor soul out of the remaining four, oblivious to my machinations, would crumble in the face of the overwhelming pressure I would bring to bear.

First I would hit them where it really hurt by cutting off the funds flowing in from the national direct mail campaign run by Parker, Dodd and Associates. Richard Parker, its founder, was a pioneer of direct mail fundraising in the service of progressive causes. He had recruited Greenpeace as one of his first clients and the income stream he had developed was the lifeblood of the San Francisco office, which was now raising over a million dollars annually. This was all happening without the approval of Vancouver, but it wasn't Richard's fault. No one had told him about the Northern Problem.

I walked unannounced into the Parker Dodd offices in the Cannery Building where Richard Parker, Bill Dodd, and their lawyer happened to be meeting. I outlined my plan. "My faction on the board is deadly serious about this," I concluded, "but there is one critical element that needs to be in place. You are raising thousands of dollars in the U.S. using the Greenpeace name, and this could be in violation of Vancouver's trademark rights. I would think that it would be prudent for you to discontinue your activities until this is all worked out. That would give San Francisco additional incentive to settle and would significantly aid our efforts." I felt proud of myself for stating my argument so forcefully. I was operating outside the rules, and it felt intoxicating. Secretly I wished the tribe could crush the opposition with one swift blow, but they couldn't and this was the next best thing.

It was their lawyer who responded. "Well, actually this is the reason I am here right now. I'm advising them that this is exactly what they should do given the legal situation."

Richard agreed. "We have a new business here with a dozen employees who are depending on us. We can't risk it all for this, so we'll certainly stop everything until things are settled."

Well, I thought, as I left their office. *I got what I wanted.* Even if it really wasn't the result of my doing, nobody will know the difference. I called Patrick Moore in Vancouver and told him of my plan to come up and negotiate a settlement. I said I had the support of two other board members and that a fourth would certainly cave in under the pressure. To demonstrate our seriousness, I added, I had gone to Parker Dodd and gotten them to cut off the fundraising so as to squeeze the renegades into submission. That should prove I wasn't just the traitorous lawyer that some in Vancouver suspected!

It seemed to impress Patrick, and the wheels were set in motion. I secretly flew up to Vancouver with Donna Scheff, one of my allies on the board, and met with Peter Ballem. We drafted an agreement that called for San Francisco to acknowledge Vancouver's ownership of the trademark and set up a joint governing body, giving Vancouver a majority by one vote, and shipped it down to San Francisco as a last ditch offer of settlement.

"Where did this come from?" the San Francisco lawyers puzzled when the proposal arrived. I couldn't exactly reveal the mystery of its origin, but a board meeting was called nonetheless to consider it.

The evening before, I stopped by my parents' house and excitedly described the events that were unfolding. I rarely told them anything about my life so they must have found it unusual that I was so animated. But as I began describing my little scheme with Parker Dodd, my mother ran into her room and threw herself on her bed. She lay there sobbing as I sheepishly finished the story for my father. She must have been crying for the whales that were being killed while we humans argued over the ownership of the name of the organization that was trying to save them. She was a big Greenpeace supporter. "How is it," she once asked me, a bit in awe, "that someone like Bob Hunter would grow up to want to risk his life to save whales?"

My mother visiting the Ohana Kai in San Francisco

The meeting was an anticlimax. I argued for accepting the settlement, along with Dick Dillman and Donna Scheff. Then it was Tom Falvey's turn. His was the swing vote. We knew the others would be against: Carole Sears, Eddie Chavies, and Gollum himself, John Frizell, who had recently migrated to San Francisco. I hadn't attempted to talk to Tom personally. There was no way we could have a serious conversation—we might as well have been from different planets. Tom stroked his long beard. "No, I can't go along with this," he pronounced. "I just don't believe it's in the best interests of Greenpeace."

That was it. My grand scheme was in ruins. I had failed.

Trying to be dramatic, I got up and announced I was therefore resigning my position as General Counsel of Greenpeace
Foundation of America.

As I was the key figure in the circumstances that led to the
establishment of the San Francisco office, the taking of my
deposition was a major event. Seven lawyers from all sides
attended. I answered their questions as honestly as I could,
believing the facts favored Vancouver's side, but of course
that didn't resolve anything. San Francisco's lawyers took the
same set of facts and wove a magnificent argument supporting their side.

Although I had resigned my paid position I was still on the
board of directors and launched a subversive battle against the
San Francisco office, becoming known as "the leak" because
I would attend strategy sessions, then phone Patrick Moore
and give him the details. Being terrible at keeping secrets, this
eventually got out and a meeting was called in an attempt to
remove me from the board—but they couldn't get a quorum.
It didn't much matter because, in the end, none of my machinations made the slightest bit of difference.

Meanwhile, San Francisco's lawyers made their own
attempt to reach a settlement with Vancouver, coming up
with an agreement very similar to the one I had negotiated.
It would have been approved if not for the last-minute inter-
vention of the only person capable of changing the course of
events.

David McTaggart, leader of Greenpeace Europe, didn't like
what he was hearing from his friends in North America. He
had no love for the Vancouver tribe, feeling they had given
him little support during his voyage to Moruroa and had then
tried to appropriate all the credit for themselves. A common
Vancouver pattern, it seemed. Someone had to put up a fight,
and since the U.S. Greenpeacers lacked leadership, that job

fell to him. Others have suggested that this was the moment of opportunity that McTaggart had been waiting for—and knew would eventually come. He flew to the United States with two of his associates, toured the offices mobilizing them against Vancouver, and then settled in San Francisco to finish the battle. His arrival at the last minute caused San Francisco to scuttle the settlement agreement their lawyers had negotiated and instead place their faith in him—with the notable, but now insignificant exception of myself.

McTaggart was convinced that the only reason I was not wholeheartedly on his side was because I was afraid of Patrick and his lawsuit. "Look, I used to be in the construction business," he confided to me alone one day. "We'll get a couple of guys, take Patrick aside and give him a little talking to. You won't have anything to worry about." Accepting his somewhat disturbing offer was of course out of the question, but I had mixed feelings about McTaggart. He seemed an unlikely environmentalist, older than the rest of us, not at all a crazy-hippie-counterculture type, but a scrappy, competitive, can-do sort of person willing to apply his boundless energy and powers of persuasion to any opportunity that came along. Greenpeace just happened to be that opportunity. I saw him as ruthless and manipulative but when he focused his intense blue eyes on you it was impossible not to yield to his charm and the force of his personality. Part of you knew you were being taken for a ride, but you also knew it would be a fabulous ride. A born leader, he made people follow without feeling they were being led. He had built a tight-knit organization in Europe focused on running environmental campaigns, avoiding the problems Vancouver faced. He knew that for Greenpeace to succeed it needed to be organized and run just like any other corporation, not like a tribe of hippies. He was not an intellectual giant or a great thinker, simply a practical genius who could make things happen—exactly the kind of leader Greenpeace craved. Perhaps, as Paul Watson himself would suggest, he was The Mule.

McTaggart's solution was simple: Vancouver must relinquish all claims to the Greenpeace name outside of Canada. At a meeting with the San Francisco board on August 1, McTaggart offered financial assistance to the San Francisco office to help defray its legal expenses. In exchange the San Francisco board would have to agree to fight, and must agree that the objective was to establish an independent Greenpeace organization in the United States free of any control from Canada. Alan Thornton, McTaggart's ally from Greenpeace U.K., added that Vancouver would have to get their own house in order, but once they gave up control of the name "we will come in and support them." Inside I was seething at the arrogance and condescension. I thought back to Hunter's description of how they felt when they walked out of the international meeting eighteen months earlier—"we're lying on our backs with our legs spread"—and now they were being asked to cut off their balls and hand them to McTaggart on a platter, and then a few dollars would be tossed their way to pay off the debts they had incurred as a result of their alleged incompetence in running their failed campaigns. But all I could do was nitpick at McTaggart's conditions. I pointed out that my objective was reconciliation with Vancouver, not a long-drawn-out fight to the finish, and that I could not agree to accept his money if it tied our hands in negotiating a settlement by committing us to a pre-ordained outcome. If McTaggart was even slightly annoyed at my obstruction, he didn't let it show.

In any case, the end came quickly. There was to be no battle to the finish, no day of reckoning. Having unified and mobilized the opposition, McTaggart headed triumphantly to

Vancouver. Despite his real antipathy toward the elders, he was originally from Vancouver himself so he could easily slip back into the role of their old drinking buddy. The principals gathered at a local pub and, without the benefit of lawyers, negotiated an end to the entire affair. Vancouver had taken its last and best shot, and it wasn't good enough. McTaggart had outmaneuvered them, and they simply hadn't the resources, or the will, to wage a long and possibly losing battle. With an air of resignation, they finally agreed to the creation of an international organization based on McTaggart's model of one country, one vote—convenient for McTaggart since he had Greenpeace offices in several European countries and the United States on his side, all of whom promptly elected him the first Chairman of Greenpeace International.

Thus ended the era of Vancouver's hegemony, or claimed hegemony, over Greenpeace. One could argue that in a way they had achieved their objective. At last an international structure had been created that would put an end to the years of chaos and strife, even if it meant turning it over to McTaggart. Not insignificantly, Vancouver would also get assistance in paying off the large debt it had run up organizing the early campaigns that put Greenpeace on the map. For San Francisco, the cost in legal fees had been over a hundred thousand dollars, but it too felt vindicated. Perhaps they had been right all along. The Vancouver group was in no position to take over Greenpeace. The lawsuit had been the last gasp of the original tribe that had been slowly withering away through attrition and fatigue. In reality only Pat Moore had stuck around to carry the torch to the final battle.

As for me, I would continue to blame myself for my failure to protect Vancouver's right to the Greenpeace name when incorporating the San Francisco office, until I realized that I was exaggerating my role in the matter. By the time I came along, San Francisco was already a buzzing hive of Greenpeace activity, already wary and resentful of Vancouver's claims of authority. Had I presented papers for them to sign giving ownership of the name to Vancouver I would doubtless have been sent packing.

Vancouver had had its moment of glory, its night in the shoebox, when all of creation was fresh and new and possibilities seemed limitless. It had opened its hands, let the power go, and it would never return. It had not been graceful, and lives would never be the same, but perhaps that was how it had to be.

Led by McTaggart, Greenpeace would experience its greatest period of growth, especially after the publicity generated when French commandos sank its ship *Rainbow Warrior* in New Zealand in 1985. He would serve for over a decade, then go into semi-retirement on doctor's orders and produce olive oil on a farm in Italy. He died in an automobile accident near his home on March 23, 2001, lionized as the Shadow Warrior, one of the giants of the environmental movement but largely unknown to the general public—one who, like Greenpeace, was never free from controversy and criticism.

Bob Hunter had already left Greenpeace, wound up working as an environmental reporter for a Toronto television station, and continued to dabble in environmental causes. He died of cancer in 2005. Patrick Moore served as the Canadian delegate to Greenpeace International for several years. Then, in what he said was reaction to some of the excesses of the environmental movement, he switched sides, becoming a spokesman for the British Columbia timber industry, an advocate for nuclear power, and a climate change denier, reviled by many as an eco-traitor.

Both the Vancouver and San Francisco Greenpeace offices became relatively insignificant as the center of Greenpeace activity shifted to Europe. Those innocents who had so eagerly thrown in their lot with McTaggart soon found that the Greenpeace they knew had ceased to exist. Its energies diffused, Greenpeace would no longer be a potent force in the public arena in the United States—nor could it ever again be accurately described as a "grassroots" organization.

Had I been smart, ambitious, or both, I might have had a lifelong career alongside McTaggart, who had tried, but failed, to recruit my support. I had scornfully burned all my bridges. There was no place for me in the new Greenpeace order and I knew it. I didn't even want it. Greenpeace was not my universe, and McTaggart was not my god. I had been an interloper in a landscape populated by extraordinary characters and dramatic events. From now on I would have to make my own way in life, like many others who had been touched by the Greenpeace magic and would forever remember those precious but fleeting moments when life overflowed with excitement, purpose, and adventure.

JENN

The Meiklejohn Country Manor stands at the corner of La Loma and La Vereda in the North Berkeley Hills. Across the street is the former Hillside Elementary School which I attended from kindergarten through fourth grade. Down at the other end of La Vereda is the house I lived in with my parents from 1963 to 1967.

Alexander Meiklejohn, my father's former teacher and mentor, would get up every day, dress in a suit and tie, and head for his study with its magnificent view looking south towards the Berkeley campus and west across the San Francisco Bay. There he would ponder and write about the subjects that had been his lifelong passions: educational reform, democracy, free speech. In 1912 he had become the youngest president of Amherst College, where he advocated the controversial view that elite Amherst should open its doors to a student body more representative of American society—including African Americans and other minorities. For this and other reasons, such as his refusal to field a football team, he was fired in 1923. He then founded a short-lived experimental college at the University of Wisconsin, the inspiration for my father's own program, before moving to Berkeley where he was to spend the rest of his life. My father met him in a philosophy class at Wisconsin, and it was this experience which led him to follow Meiklejohn to Berkeley and pursue a PhD in philosophy. By

the 1960s, when Meiklejohn was in his nineties, his prom-
inence had begun to fade. Although he was awarded the
Presidential Medal of Freedom by President Kennedy, he is
now largely forgotten, as those who were touched by his brilliance have themselves passed on. As for me, my contact with
the great man was limited to the times I would come over
to help his wife Helen balance their checkbook and perform
other household chores.

Meiklejohn died on a cold December day in 1964. When
he got the news, my father broke down in tears. It was the
only time I ever saw him cry. Helen lived on for almost twenty
more years. I am told she suffered from Alzheimer's although
I never visited the house after Alec died. But on the morning
of May 19, 1983, I happened to be driving by and noticed it
was open for realtors to inspect as it was soon to be placed
on the market. I parked, walked inside, and was greeted by
a perky young realtor named Jenn. She didn't know me, but
this was the third time I had encountered her. The first time
I had been out for dinner with a friend who leaned across
the table and pointed her out to me in a hushed voice. The
next time I was visiting another open house. She was sitting
in the living room absorbed in her own thoughts, barely
glancing at me as if I didn't exist. But this time was different.
Her perkiness focused instantly on me. "You don't look like
a realtor," she remarked playfully. Well, technically I was. As
an attorney, I was entitled under California law to take the
Realtors exam and be licensed as a broker despite having
no experience whatsoever in the field. She offered me some
chocolate covered strawberries and I ate as many as I could
without appearing to be greedy.

Jenn and I flirted quite blatantly. I explained my history
with the Meiklejohn Country Manor, as she called it in her
marketing brochure. I thought that was a little tacky but kept

quiet. Doubtless Meiklejohn would have found this whole yuppie business which was manifesting itself in the 1980s quite distasteful; he abhorred all aspects of materialism. Jenn herself might have passed as a yuppie. Her personal style she described as "sporty," she drove a BMW and explained to me that she got started in real estate because she wanted to understand how money got moved around. I mentioned that I was in the process of selling the house on Grizzly Peak that I had lived in with my first two wives. I had listed it myself as a "FSBO" (for sale by owner), and I invited her to come by and take a look. This was my lure.

Jenn came over to inspect my house and we wound up making a date for lunch at Chez Panisse, of Alice Water's fame. Over appetizers I happened to spill that I was currently dating a woman named Amelia. It was true. And I liked Amelia a lot. Being with her was very comfortable. She was a nurse, an uncomplicated nurturing sort of person. We had gone on a trip to Hawaii and had a wonderful relaxing time. There was no reason I should want to dump her. Except that Jenn was very different. She was exciting, full of energy, a real challenge, a real catch. Learning of her competitor, Jenn turned to the waiter and said, "Bring me another glass of wine, I've just met Amelia!" Of course, Jenn knew she would have no trouble getting me to send Amelia packing, which is exactly what happened.

As for Jenn, she had broken up with her longtime boyfriend Randall, like me the son of a UC professor and a successful international drug smuggler (wildly more successful than me; he drove a Ferrari, I only had a Porsche). Jenn had tired of the fact that Randall was never home and was seeking a less peripatetic boyfriend. She had gone through several who had proved unsatisfactory, so she was open to someone like me who looked pretty good and was an attorney to boot.

After our lunch she invited me over to her house, a beautiful Edwardian flat in the Rockridge neighborhood, and cooked an elaborate Thai dinner. It was the first time we made love but the last time she cooked an elaborate meal. We resolved to go away to Mendocino for the weekend to see if we were really meant for each other. I found it very exhausting; Jenn required a lot of engagement. There was not a moment of respite from the intense attention, which was laser focused on me, demanding attention in return. For an introvert like me that was very draining. But we happened to run into an older couple who had been clients of hers. They invited us over to their spectacular house overlooking the ocean and snapped a photo of us sitting on a sofa. They sent us the photo and Jenn and I stared at it in disbelief. We looked so good together. That photo sealed our fate and by the fourth of July Jenn had moved in with me.

My home at the time was a beautiful Spanish-style bungalow set high above the street on Colorado Avenue in the North Berkeley hills, light and airy and surrounded by greenery. Of all the places I have lived before and after it was my favorite. It had previously been rented by two female graduate students in psychology, one of whom—Deborah—had been my girlfriend. We had met three years earlier at a party given by her mutual friend Susan, who I knew from the dorms at UC. She had beautiful blond hair and blue eyes, the freshest Wisconsin skin and was wearing yellow overalls and a purple silk shirt. Alone in the backyard, we looked in each other's eyes and kissed. She later told me she had resolved that summer of 1980 to find a boyfriend, and I was the lucky one.

Being a psychologist Deborah was very excited thinking perhaps she had finally met a true *puer*.

Puer aeternus (Latin for "eternal boy")...in mythology

is a child-god who is forever young. In the analytical psychology of Carl Jung, the term is used to describe an older person whose emotional life has remained at an adolescent level, which is also known as "Peter Pan syndrome," a more recent pop-psychology label. In Jung's conception, the *puer* typically leads a "provisional life" due to the fear of being caught in a situation from which it might not be possible to escape. He or she covets independence and freedom, opposes boundaries and limits, and tends to find any restriction intolerable...The shadow of the *puer* is the *senex* (Latin for "old man"), associated with the god Cronus—disciplined, controlled, responsible, rational, ordered. Conversely, the shadow of the *senex* is the *puer,* related to Hermes or Dionysus—unbounded instinct, disorder, intoxication, whimsy...Like all archetypes, the *puer* is bipolar, exhibiting both a "positive" and a "negative" aspect. The "positive" side of the *puer* appears as the Divine Child who symbolizes newness, potential for growth, hope for the future. He also foreshadows the hero that he sometimes becomes (e.g. Heracles). The "negative" side is the child-man who refuses to grow up and meet the challenges of life face on, waiting instead for his ship to come in and solve all his problems." (Wikipedia)

Whether or not I was a true *puer*, I knew I was not a *senex*. But I definitely needed therapy, so Deborah set me up with the wife of her own therapist who I was to see on and off for several years, mostly to no avail. Once a *puer*, always a *puer.*

Deborah was a member of the Jungian Society and took me to a lecture which explained a lot. It had to do with the stages of a relationship. Phase One is the falling in love part, where everything is new and magical. Just the kind of thing a *puer* likes. Phase Two is the disillusionment, where the magic wears off and you fall back to Earth. *Puers* do not like that phase. Finally, for healthy people, Phase Three follows, the stage of integration where you resolve the contradictions of phases one and two and forge a healthy relationship based in reality. *Puers* never get to that stage.

After two years Deborah completed her PhD and was offered a teaching position at the University of Texas. We drove with all her belongings in a U Haul truck towing her Fiat station wagon to Austin, after which I flew back to Berkeley and moved myself into the charming Colorado Avenue house which I had inherited from her. Our parting had been sad but inevitable. I was not about to follow her to Austin and, unlike my previous relationships, she was not about to beg, plead and bludgeon me into marriage. Definitely the healthiest of my girlfriends to date, I felt I owed her a lot for helping me to become if only slightly healthier. Wistfully she once expressed the hope that we could have had something "just regular," but she probably understood that was contrary to my nature. I would continue to have fond feelings for Deborah for the rest of my life.

Deborah gone, I now entered Phase One with the house. I painted the walls white, waxed the beautiful oak floors, and got a resale permit so I could pose as a decorator and purchase a beautiful linen sofa and other furnishings from the Kreiss Collection in San Francisco's Design Center. I subscribed to Architectural Digest to get decorating ideas and by the time I was finished had prepared a fine nest into which I could lure an unsuspecting young female who hadn't been to any Jung lectures. Jenn was to be that female.

Our first year together had its ups and downs. After moving in Jenn put her stamp on my beloved little house, but it was acceptable. I endured the dreaded ritual of being introduced to her friends (I had few I felt I could introduce her to) and we shopped for new clothes to give me a sportier image. The ups were attributable to the high we experienced falling in love. As in the photo, people found us a handsome couple, especially because we seemed so into each other. When we held hands, which was most of the time, people could sense the intoxicating flow of energy between us. Jenn left little notes for me every morning before she trotted off to sell people hopes and dreams in the form of new houses, giving me my assignments for the day, each note signed with a lipstick kiss.

For her birthday on November 8th, we decided to take a trip to Mexico. It had always been my dream to stay at Las Brisas, a romantic hotel in Acapulco consisting of little casitas carved into a hillside each with its own private pool. They had pink Jeeps you could borrow if you wanted to make an excursion outside the grounds, but Acapulco itself had little charm. I jumped naked into our pool for a dip, enjoying the view of the ocean and feeling caressed by the warm water. We went to dinner, but it was disconcerting. As we sat there alone a vague unacknowledged sense of discomfort clouded over us for we could think of little to say to each other. Could things have gone dry that quickly?

After a few days at Las Brisas we rented a car and drove up to Zihuatanejo, staying in an old hotel by the ocean run by a German family. Compared to Acapulco, Zihuatanejo was lovely. We would walk from the hotel into town for dinners of pescado al mojo de ajo, passing a deserted mega mansion supposedly built by a cartel member.

Vacation over, we headed to the local airport only to discover our flight had been delayed. My sense of discomfort magnified. The pictures I took of Jenn while waiting told the tale. She had a pensive faraway look as if trying to restrain some inner distress. I imagined her feeling deeply unhappy

and thinking she had made a huge mistake with this relationship, but I dared not say anything.

Back in Berkeley, it was easy to ignore the warning signs.
Jenn was always busy at work, and I was good at ignoring
problems. We decided we would get married on May 19th,
1984, exactly one year after we met. A couple of times we
discussed doubts about going through with it but no, I said,
it would be too sad if we didn't. Once a friend questioned
my decision and I responded forcefully that Jenn was what
I wanted. But I remember thinking as I said it, *Is that really
true?* I knew I once had thought it, but was that just a passing
fancy, powerful as it had seemed? Pushing all doubts aside,
we plunged ahead with our plans.

May 19th was a beautiful sunny spring day at the Madrona
Manor, a Victorian bed and breakfast outside the town of
Healdsburg in Sonoma County. It was there that we had
decided to hold the wedding, and a beautiful wedding it was,
the clear favorite of my four. I drove up from Berkeley that
morning in my ratty old Porsche. My parents were there and
it was to be one of the last times I would see my mother. My
mother liked Jenn. "She's so lively!" she had enthused. What
sealed her affection was that when offered a look at my child-
hood photos Jenn had at least feigned interest. My previous
wife had not. Jenn's parents were also there, although they
had long ago divorced. Her mother was a retired Alameda
County jailer, her father an eccentric artist who lived in Santa
Cruz and wrote cryptic letters containing riddles that caused
Jenn to burst into tears.

Putting on my dorky looking white suit in the dressing
area set aside for us, I found myself choking up. "It's very
emotional," I said to my best man Gary, my old friend from
Greenpeace. The ceremony was quite simple. We wrote no
special vows, gave no speeches, invited no friends or family to

address the group. But most importantly for me, the food was spectacular. The pastry chef had worked at Chez Panisse and baked a glorious cake with layers of fresh strawberries.

That night we retired to a hotel room in downtown Healdsburg as there had been no room at the inn for us. Alone together, we tried our best to rekindle the spark that once animated our time together. For me it was a painful effort which failed to live up to expectations. But we soldiered through.

On to the honeymoon! I had planned it, and it was a disaster. For some reason I settled on the Sheraton Hotel on Molokai, the one Hawaiian island I had never visited. The hotel was plastic and dreary and there was nothing to do on the island except visit the old leper colony. After a few thankfully short days we flew over to Maui where I rented the same condo I had stayed in with Amelia a little over a year before and with Celeste back in the early 70s. I never mentioned this to Jenn. There was nothing much to do there except explore the lavish new Hyatt Regency Hotel at Kaanapali where we bought matching red windbreaker jackets. From there we drove down the west coast of Maui, the route you aren't supposed to take, to the Hana Kai Hotel in Hana. I had stayed there before with Celeste and again with the trio of Greenpeacers I had accompanied in my effort to show my devotion to the dying Cindy Baker. Lying in bed listening to the surf outside the window as I had done years before, I wondered where all the magic I had once experienced with Jenn had gone.

THE WORLD MUST NOT FADE

It was soon after the honeymoon that my mother died while traveling alone in Turkey and Greece. In recent years she had fallen in love with those countries, especially Turkey, even learning to speak and write Turkish. Her restless wanderings are described in her journal, and the letters and postcards she sent to my father on her final trip.

Bodrum, Turkey

"To understand an alien phenomenon requires an effort not only of the intellect but of the imagination".
—George Orwell

Reason and emotion—One must *feel* Turkey first. I arrive by small boat from Kos—almost in the wake of tradition, reversing the Western flow. The cool sea breeze, the salt on ones lips, clear skies without dimension—the illusion of immobility and the changing sea, preluded the night before by the Turkish moon over Greece—a crescent with the planet (Mars?) within its curve. The dry hills of Turkey form shadows lining the horizon—gradually expanding into color. Imagination peoples the crests with early Greeks—sentinels of the past—and then the Mongolian hordes, the Crusaders—the aggressive stance of conquerors and the apprehensive scan of prospective conquered. The great fort piled high with stones from the mausoleum—tomb made into fort made into museum.

Bodrum—in close perspective, quickly dispelling dream into a reality of dust, darting cats and dogs, pressing crowds, women in pantaloons and veils, women in shorts and halters (the past persevering for how long against the seductive onslaughts of the present?) Sheep folded together—tomorrow's slaughter—a religious festival. Does God wash the blood from his hands? Must his creatures all be part of an enormous cannibalism? A cycle of devouring and being devoured? When does one learn to accept this? Only in the face of the reality of death—when today's life is only a short postponement of tomorrow's death—and in the reality of rebirth? When the essence transcends its ephemeral forms? When will God reveal this to us? Why does He prolong our suffering? Or is the message revealed everywhere and we have eyes but do not see? (Christ to disciples—"they have eyes but see not.") One sees the external and suddenly a pattern forms from a series of sights—the *eye* (*nazar*) amulet bought in the marketplace; the floor of the pension—blue white and black, swirls of blue with black dots like nebula—a primordial eye; and across the street, on the white-washed walls of the house, again the eye, solidified and transfixed. Chaos—movement towards form—form—and then dissipation. But the cycle persists.

The simple pension rebuking a mode of life built on excess. At first strange and quickly becoming natural.

Between here and the sea a steppe of flat roofs (like North Africa and Portugal) and chimneys like the Algarve—unfinished minarets. Matching the sounds with the forms—children's voices, high-pitched, sheep bleating, the grunt and growl of trucks straining up the hill, motorbikes, horns honking—modern and ancient sounds. At night dogs and before dawn roosters. Man's voices guttural...

But what sound from the Cyprus rising on the hill from behind a broken stone wall? That voice—would it be more beautiful, more poignant? Part of the unheard, unsung music of the universe.

So hot and dry and dusty—but the sea cools the eye.

We are born into consciousness to know that we must die before we learn that life is a greater pain than this first knowledge. We deny this cycle—that everything feeds on everything else—imagining an alternative—Paradise—where nothing dies, where the lion lies down with the lamb...

The Black Sea—Today the sea is green. The sky is clear and blue. The hills are shadows. Without books, without memories, the sea persists—a primeval occurrence—and everything else has disappeared, the antique ships all ephemeral phenomena. Sinop—the birthplace of Diogenes—who already found the stone walls ancient. What did his lamp reveal when the shadows fell away? Was he caught in the net of his two eyes? (The sun is the world's eye). Dazed by the light of his lamp? Will I find a different truth from him? That life is very short—that age and death defeats everything? Life a brief succession of moments?

One must pass beyond the three obvious dimensions in order to understand. I hope that in this life I can see beyond. From the very beginning I wanted to know. I knew that I must know. God said Ask, and thou shalt receive. Understanding was what I asked for.

Sinop—a quiet like the past. Fishing boats, men repairing nets, houses crumbling, falling down the hills. There is something I vaguely remember—some ancient conquest, some site. Does my memory belong to everyone—universal memory—or is it a personal edifice?

Dreams—symbolism very strange, so meaningful. The snake, the black bull. Consciously unthought, unspoken. My heart is full of pain, my mouth full of lies, my mind full of illusions. Self like the ocean—always the same, always changing, energy moving through form. The moon's energy moves through me, weaker and weaker. Is there another force?

At night narrow unlit winding steep steps of stone, small shops open to the alleys.

Istanbul—This alien world becomes less alien. The revulsions wane and return in tides. The wind rustling knots of dirty plastic in the streets. Soot etched centimeter by centimeter into stone. Constricted alleys burdened with old buildings. Veiled women crouched on the stones amidst children, hanging out of balconies. What movements, what gestures create the present? What sounds? Only the machine is the Present. It overwhelms, destroys every vestige of the past. Outside the hotel the rooster still crows. The phenomena of the present—Byzantine colonnades whipped by shreds of newspaper, enduring a climate of pollution. Who remembers the future?

Istanbul must be defined by centuries, by thousands of ciphers. I know only myself. How many ages am I and

why do I remember nothing? Perhaps to learn everything over and over, always from a new facet—but what
does it add up to? My character?

I must learn to feel—why did I feel so much and now
I am like the memory of a flame—where is the flame
itself? Are we constantly dying in this life?

Strolling along the street the constant beep of taxis—
onslaught of trucks, buses, automobiles—waves of
shadows. Man who passes so quickly.

The university amidst Moslem mosques, gravestones,
pigeons, cats. Huge portal—Arabic inscriptions. Old
libraries. Bazaar leading into corridors, mazes. Feelings—
revulsion, fascination, numbness, acceptance, curiosity.
Where have I exhausted myself? Not insanity because
insanity derives from much emotion.

The Turks are kind people. The Greeks are bellicose—
perhaps because they are free, and the Turks are not. A
politics of sensation—is no politics.

Ferryboat to Uskudur, where the Golden Horn,
Marmara, and Bosporus meet.

The ancient cities grew and grew and then—what is
the future? It can be dreamed.

In the hotel—people sitting blankly for hours in the
lobby: frenzied children, Egyptians, Libyans, Spaniards,
Germans, Americans, English. Turkish clerks. Quibbles
over checks. Beautiful Libyan girls. Everyone is waiting,
standing around picking teeth. Men greet each other
with kisses on each cheek. I am in the midst and yet
I am not here—because I belong to so many pasts, so
many places, so many worlds—but to what people? My
memory must not blank out. Vision must not fade. The
world must not fade. Music, sound, is a memory—many
memories—the cries of street vendors.

The Turkish street is alive—cats, men, vendors, cars, shouts, arguments—much activity but little results, little effects.

Mind must replace emotion...

Greece—Gray skies and seas, slow heaving movements, the clouds, the waves, the ferryboat. The sun dim through a relentless haze. November already—everything is heaviness. Oil tanker moored on Athens bay, behind Piraeus, Athens in a dull retreat. Inside the ferryboat Greeks with their meals of chicken, bread, spread out on sacks before them. The faces etched by labor, pressed between closed spaces, clinging to the inside of the boat. The young men on deck, breaking their energies over each other—already caught in the traps their past has constructed for them.

Where is the creativity, the beauty, the thought of Greece today? Masculine energies, burnt up in speeding cars. The illusions and masks of masculinity—an endless chain of cigarettes, the expanding paunch weighing down the man. The woman—heavy with children, thickened waists, pendulous breasts—perhaps the only strength of Greece. Finished—polarized politics, polarized hates.

May 26, 1984, Athens, Greece

Dearest Joe—I wasn't intending to write you any letters—but I miss you—and even if you don't read them, just by writing I have the feeling of talking to you.

The plane ride wasn't too difficult this time and my only jet lag symptom is that I feel sleepy. I felt very depressed on the plane and yesterday, my first day. Fortunately, I made the decision to come to

Athens—not Piraeus. At the airport yesterday (and on the plane) huge crowds of tourists…The airport manager for TWA noticed me and immediately followed me around helping me. He found me a lovely hotel in Athens (about $13 a day) with a beautiful roof garden with a view of the Acropolis—right on the edge of the Plaka (old Athens). He also carried my bags to a bus that goes directly to Athens—so I paid only about 60 cents instead of six dollars for a taxi. This is a 100% improvement on the Omni Hotel. The tourists in this hotel are mostly English, French, Scandinavian couples—very nice. I had a nice walk in the Plaka this evening. The weather is *perfect*—the best I've ever experienced here—warm sun and steady cool breeze. The air is much cleaner.

I'm very concerned about my digestion. On the plane I read *East-West* magazine about the macrobiotic diet and food balance. Since I *know* that it cured Carl Dibble of cancer I'm more or less convinced that it could help me. At least I have put myself on a diet—I must lose. Today I hardly ate. Joe, you also must watch your diet. *Chew* your food also—it's really a matter of choosing life or death.

May 28, 1984, Athens, Greece

I decided to stay first few days in Athens instead of Piraeus. My little hotel here has roof garden with view of Parthenon. Trip OK. No jet lag. Last night ate a salad at taverna in old section of city. Danced at a Greek wedding! Everyone surprised at my dancing. I haven't made any plans yet. Today will decide. Probably to Samos. Feel a little bad. Take care of yourself.

May 30, 1984, Samos, Greece

Arrived in Samos! (Home of Pythagoras). The town where I'm staying is quite tranquil—not as nice as Kos—but pretty. I'm hoping to make a tour of the island, also get in some swimming. Food quite good—the specialty is octopus! But I'm hardly eating—both to lose weight and to help my digestion. *Please please* eat slower, eat less, and eat mainly vegetables. Keep in good health. Water the plants because they cry when they're dry. From here I'll go to the island of Chios, then to Thessaloniki or Kavala.

May 31, 1984, Samos, Greece

Still on island of Samos. Found a hotel right on the water—very nice for $8.00 a day. I just had my first swim. The water is perfect and I feel much better. I haven't been sick—only very depressed (for a long time). The town of Samos is not as nice as the town of Kos—but the whole island is lovely. Very quiet—people friendly. Many American, German, French tourists. Food good but I'm trying very hard not to eat very much. Of course I took too much. There is windsurfing here. I might try it. Will probably stay here at least till June 4, then I will go to Chios and Lesbos—then to N. Greece by boat—Kavala—then by bus or train to Istanbul. *Take care of yourself!*

June 2, 1984, Samos, Greece

I forgot to mail this in Athens. Right now I'm staying at the Surfside Hotel in Samos. Its right at the water—lovely swimming! The air is balmy and fresh. The woman who owns the hotel is American married to a Greek. They have a couple of dogs and a really goofy cat named Boo Boo who seems to run the place. I feel well—my digestion is better—only am *covered* with mosquito bites. The food is very good. I'm sticking to vegetarian diet, *trying* to eat less and walk a lot. A little lonely—met a woman who studied 7 years at Berkeley—and knows where Florida Street is. Samos Island is really beautiful—home of Pythagoras, once largest Greek city before Athens.

I intend to leave Samos Monday for the Island of Chios (not Kos).

June 6, 1984, Izmir, Turkey

I just came from Samos by boat to Kusadasi and to Izmir. Tomorrow I go to Istanbul. Samos was beautiful and I had wonderful swims. Even you would like Samos. The Greeks there were very friendly—it was like paradise. However, I was "alone in Heaven." Made friends with the many dogs and cats. Everyone lives in harmony—but unfortunately a war shadow on the horizon. Islands heavily militarized. It is getting quite hot now. I might go back to Samos later—but I should try another island. So far, trip fine. The swimming cures my depression. My digestion much better. Food everywhere very good—but I'm trying to lose. Take good care of yourself. *Walk*—don't eat too much.

June 9, 1984, Buyukada, Turkey

Today I went to this island in the Sea of Marmara—about an hour from Istanbul by boat and rode all around the island in horse drawn buggy—no cars allowed here. Very beautiful. Formerly sultan's relatives exiled here—many beautiful old wooden homes.

(Later [Istanbul]) Today I went to see Pierre Loti's famous café on a hill behind Istanbul and then to the famous Eyüp Mosque—it is Ramazan and nobody eats (openly) during the day. Food good but am *trying* to lose. So far, health very good—only mosquitoes bother me. No problems but prices high—cherries more than a dollar a pound, sometimes. I must find cheaper hotel. Tomorrow I will go to the Black Sea and try to swim. I miss you—you had better miss me. Time seems to pass slowly but trip is very interesting. Hard to find newspapers so I don't have too good an idea of what is happening there.

June 16, 1984, Sile, Turkey

I am now in Sile, Turkey—a village on the Black Sea. Name means "wild flower." There are many here. The Black Sea hills are beautiful—forested, green. However, the sea is very cold—like the ocean near S.F. I still go swimming. You were right—a small place by the sea is best. I have eaten something that has made me feel a bit dizzy, nauseated, the last few days—however, a little better now. Everyone here in the village is nice. This whole month is Ramazan—therefore no people—no tourists hardly. June is a very good month to travel— next month there will be many crowds everywhere by the sea. My Turkish is greatly improved—but still difficult. Everyone very surprised I can speak. Fruit expensive but very good—strawberries like Japanese farmer in

Santa Barbara. I don't know where I'll go next—but back to Greece soon. Love to you.

June 20, 1984, Istanbul, Turkey

I am in Istanbul and trying to decide where to go next. I will try to go to Troy—then on to Greece. So far everything fine. I spent a week in a Black Sea village—Sile—and swam a lot. I had a wonderful day there—danced Turkish folk dances—and in the evening watched The Argonaut sail into the harbor. Ate a fish dinner on a terrace above the sea. Beautiful green countryside, many wild flowers, 500 year old tree. However—looking forward to coming home.

June 25, 1984, Ayvalik, Turkey

I finally got to Troy—a rather difficult trip by boat and bus—two nights at the Dardanelles. Very sad because of all the graves. People say there is still a smell of death. Then on to Troy—all alone there. A very interesting experience. Only wildflowers, lizards and birds alive there now. After that I went to Pergamos—also very interesting. At Asklepion I drank at the sacred spring and ran along the sacred corridor—saw the museum. Now am in Ayvalik in Turkey—a village on the Aegean near Lesbos. Tomorrow I'll take a boat to Lesbos. I will later try to get to Israel. Health good. I have seen so many things—Ayvalik sad because once Greek—beautiful old Greek buildings in ruin—church now a mosque. Every night I eat sardines (like Portugal), rice, salad, watermelon. I saw real camel caravans!

07/12/84   06:22
MR. JOSEPH TUSSMAN
74 FLORIDA AVENUE
BERKELEY, CALIFORNIA 94707
WITH DEEP REGRET, THE AMERICAN
EMBASSY IN ATHENS, GREECE INFORMS
YOU OF THE DEATH OF YOUR WIFE, MRS.
LORRIE SHADBOLT TUSSMAN ON JULY 11,
1984. ACCORDING TO SYGROU HOSPITAL,
ATHENS, HER CAUSE OF DEATH HAS NOT YET
BEEN DETERMINED. WE HAVE IDENTIFIED
HER THROUGH HER PASSPORT...
WE EXTEND OUR DEEPEST SYMPATHY
TO YOU AND YOUR FAMILY IN YOUR
BEREAVEMENT.
AMERICAN EMBASSY, ATHENS, GREECE

My mother in Turkey

The facts are murky, but it appears my mother had some kind of injury. I imagine her scrambling around a rocky beach, losing her footing and scraping her leg. Her usual remedy for such a thing was to rub olive oil on it. Whatever it was led to an infection and a case of septic shock, her whole body turning a bright red. She was taken on a long ambulance ride to Athens where, checking into the hospital, she was asked if she wanted her family to be contacted. She said no. That night she died in her room of an apparent embolism.

My reaction to my mother's death was muted. As my friend Deborah said when I told her about it, in some way it might have been a relief, as there was little likelihood that we would ever resolve the gulf between us. Both of us were too reserved and introverted. Once when Deborah and I were at a movie, I noticed in horror that my mother was seated two rows behind us. We both pretended not to notice each other. Another time Deborah and I were having ice cream sundaes at Sweet Dreams when I spotted my mother at an adjoining table. Again, we carefully avoided each other.

B ack in Berkeley after the honeymoon, Jenn's next project took shape. The house that we were living in was a
mere rental and as a realtor Jenn felt it imperative that
she should own the house she lived in. She began a search for
our new residence, dragging me to see several houses, all of
which I hated. Finally, she settled on an older brown shingle
duplex on Arch Street near what was then called Berkeley's
Gourmet Ghetto. Jenn arranged to find new tenants for the
Colorado Avenue house; they really annoyed me because they
seemed so blasé about what had been my precious little jewel
box.

Moving to Arch Street was maybe not the straw that broke
the camel's back, but it certainly gave it a good strain. The
house needed a lot of work as it had been owned by an elderly
couple who had raised their family there but never made any
upgrades. The walls were covered with horrible wallpaper
which I was assigned the task of removing. I spent entire days
scraping away only to have Jenn come home, carefully inspect
my work, and find little flaws. Living in chaos with workers
constantly traipsing around was not something that agreed
with my personality.

There was one bright spot. Jenn decided that getting a
kitten would help our relationship. The parents of her former
beau Randall happened to have a litter and Jenn asked them

to pick a special one for us. That special one we named Nobby, a delightful little creature who I grew to love dearly.

Speaking of Randall, he was soon to get married himself. To my chagrin he had remained a presence in Jenn's life, using a post office box she rented as his personal mail drop. It made me so upset that one day while Jenn was on the phone with him, I began pulling dishes out of the kitchen cabinet and breaking them in a ridiculous display of jealousy. Although she had left him because of his absences, at least when he was present he was "present," Jenn needled. The implication was that even when I was present, I was absent.

Jenn and I were both invited to the wedding held at Randall's parents' house high in the Berkeley Hills. It was a typical wedding for an international drug dealer. Randall's large semi-truck, used I assumed to transport loads of marijuana, was parked in the road outside, something not normally seen in this neighborhood. The caterer had been advised of the location for the wedding only that morning so as not to tip anyone off. A large stage had been constructed in the back yard for dancing and musical performances by flamenco artists. Bottles of Chateau Margaux flowed freely accompanied by juicy racks of lamb. Guests included famed environmentalist David Brower and other colorful characters whose background was best not inquired into. As for Randall's wife, Jenn had speculated that Randall had only married her because he was upset that Jenn had gotten married before him and to someone else. Randall probably wondered why Jenn had chosen me.

On another occasion Jenn and I were invited to the house of a realtor friend of hers, Deborah Ritchie. I remembered Deborah from a prior life when she was a teaching assistant in a comparative literature class where I was amazed by her brilliance. I would encounter her again when she was dating Vardan, Price's friend, before he landed in jail in Amsterdam. But now it was 1984 and on a dresser in Deborah's bedroom was a striking photograph of her younger self. She reminded me of one of those stylish Carnaby Street girls from London circa 1966 wearing a simple short dress with straight blond hair epitomizing that time of innocence and eternal youth.

Back in the living room Jenn was to approach me with some interesting news. Deborah had confronted her with the question, "Why in the world did you marry David Tussman?" My only response to this news was a feeble grunt, but it was a good question.

One day Jenn confided to me that what she sought in a mate was someone she could "lean on." Inwardly I recoiled in horror. The last thing I wanted was someone leaning on me, nor did I have any interest in leaning on someone myself. In confirmation Jenn once took us to take vocational aptitude tests and I scored very low on nurturance and succorance.

Then there were the boxing gloves given to us as a wedding gift, I suppose to suggest that fighting was a healthy part of a relationship. In this I had no interest My parents fought a lot, pointlessly, the issue being my father's desire for my mother to serve as a traditional faculty wife and host gracious dinner parties for his colleagues, something she resisted ferociously. There was no compromising on this; my father didn't believe in compromise. To him it was just another example of the encroachment of the model of the marketplace into all other aspects of life. Eventually he just gave up and accepted living as the schlepper he was. But because of his intellect and charisma he was able to attract a series of women who he never lived with or married but fulfilled his need for female companionship. He never divorced my mother; their relationship became more like one of father and daughter, each having

separate rooms and separate lives. He may have felt an obligation to take care of her, but he obviously loved her. After her
death he told me, "always remember the good things about
Lorrie."

Others could sense things were not right with Jenn and me.
There was a party at my law office. Jenn arrived late wearing
a ridiculous shiny sequin blouse. Her lateness and the blouse
both annoyed me. A guest made some cutting remark about
something, and I took it kind of personally. Jenn chastised me
saying he was just "playing" with me. I didn't like her idea of
play. Leaving the party our friend Yoav presaged that we were
headed for trouble.

Other things started to annoy me: Jenn's voice, which
was harsh and staccato, the fact that the phone was always
ringing, her unrelenting pushiness. But eventually it became
clear to me why I had been so attracted to her. She had something I wanted, something I lacked, something that through
association with her I might acquire. That was the element
of success, something that had eluded me since my days of
drug-dealing. Jenn and all her yuppie friends were making
lots of money, buying houses, building successful lives. And
what was I doing? My drug dealing funds had just about run
out. After Greenpeace I had opened my own law office in
downtown Berkeley specializing in advising nonprofit organizations, but that had not proved to be especially profitable.

Miraculously, the answer soon presented itself. After
buying my first personal computer, I got the idea of writing
a program to do my own client billing. After two weeks I
taught myself enough programming to get started and soon
imagined I could sell my program to other attorneys. A friend
of Jenn's had started his own software company marketing
a program he had written. *I can do that!* I thought. It took
me over a year of endless hours in front of the computer. It

helped that I was a good typist, knew some basic accounting, and had gotten the highest grade in a course in logic. It turned out that programming was just applied logic. I named it The Tussman Program, a whimsical nod to my father's program of the same name.

Jenn must have thought that my new obsession was perfectly consistent with her evaluation of my personality. She had become interested in the Enneagram, a theory of personality supposedly derived from the Sufis in which everyone can be categorized as one of nine different personality types. A woman named Helen Palmer put on programs where she would gather examples of a type and have them describe what it's like. Jenn took me to a presentation on type Five, The Observer, of which she had concluded I was an example.

> Observers believe they must protect themselves from a world that demands too much and gives too little. Consequently, Observers seek self-sufficiency and are non-demanding, analytic, thoughtful, and unobtrusive; they also can be withholding, detached, and overly private...Fives are content-focused, clear, analytical and wordy, but not big on small talk. Others may perceive Fives as emotionally disconnected, aloof, over-analytical, and distant...[They] detach from feelings and observe rather than participate. (narrativeenneagram.org)

It all seemed to make sense. Jenn, on the other hand, was clearly a Three.

> Threes are self-assured, attractive, and charming. Ambitious, competent, and energetic, they can also be status-conscious and highly driven for advancement. (www.enneagraminstitute.com)

Doubtless I was hoping some of Jenn's threeness would rub off on me and result in a successful outcome for my new business.

My product launch took place at the annual State Bar convention in San Diego in the fall of 1985. I set up my humble display in the vendor hall hoping to lure some innocent attorneys into being my first customers. There were a handful who took the bait, but I quickly realized I had to completely rewrite the program to accommodate their wishes and demands. This launched me into an endless cycle of revision and improvement of the program, adding new features and fixing bugs, while at the same time supporting my growing list of customers and trying to acquire new ones. To make a sale, I would have to visit a law office in person and demo the program. Because I was a lawyer myself, other lawyers assumed, rightly or wrongly, that I knew what I was doing. This gave me the needed edge to make a sale. For the first few years, I was constantly travelling, flying to Los Angeles, my major market, almost every week. All of this I did on my own with no help from anyone, typical of a Five. Quickly, this would take over my life and I would give up the practice of law.

On the way back from the San Diego bar convention Jenn and I had a painful conversation. I floated the proposition that perhaps we should consider splitting up as things just didn't seem to be working. My reasons were pretty vague, and Jenn seemed quite upset by it all so I put the matter on hold. It wasn't too long before I got an equally painful letter from Jenn detailing her frustrations with our marriage, stating that things had to change but expressing little hope that they would. When, as predicted, things didn't change I received the final notice. I would have to move out by the end of December 1986 as Jenn had arranged for a woman to move in on January 1st who was to be her new roommate.

I tried to savor our remaining moments as much as possible, but they were few. For my fortieth birthday Jenn took me to Masa's, then the hottest restaurant in San Francisco. It was a lovely meal, but we knew the gaiety was an illusion.

Before the appointed deadline I succeeded in subletting a carriage house in Sausalito suitable for myself and Nobby, of whom I got custody. It wasn't long before I started dating the woman who was to become my fourth wife. Busy with her and my programming projects, I quickly forgot about Jenn and she forgot about me. But six months after our separation both of us experienced a desire to reconnect. We went out to dinner, made love a couple of times, even toyed with the idea of getting back together, but neither of us had enough faith that it could work.

After our last dinner we found ourselves sitting in my car in front of my Colorado Avenue house. (Yes, the blasé tenants had moved out and I had succeeded in renting it back.) I was hoping that Jenn would come inside and we would make love. Instead, she delivered to me the news that she had just met the man who was to become her next husband and the father of her children. We held hands and for the last time I felt that powerful flow of energy that had once drawn us together. I ached inside knowing that when I let go of her hand I would be abruptly cut off from that energy. And I was right. In that instant it was over, forever.

THE TREE OF THE WIND

I t is April 2001. The phone rings. "David, this is Juan." It
had been almost thirty years since we last spoke and yet he
addressed me as if that could have been yesterday. There
was no mistaking his voice—deep, deliberate, with an aristocratic timbre. "We need to set up a new organization and
I was told you were a lawyer who specializes in nonprofits."

"Yes, that is true," I responded, equally matter-of-factly. "I
don't practice law anymore, but I can certainly help."

I had last seen Juan in 1971, when Celeste and I visited an
exhibition of colorful yarn paintings created by the Huichol
Indians of Mexico that Juan had organized in a small gallery
in Berkeley. We listened spellbound as Juan gave intricate
explanations of the symbolic meanings behind each of the
paintings. Juan had been introduced to the Huichol when his
father took him to an exhibit of yarn paintings at the Basilica
of Zapopan outside Guadalajara. He had been so impressed
that he decided he had to meet the artists who had created
them. To this point yarn paintings had been regarded merely
as indigenous handicrafts and the creators were anony-
mous. Juan felt they deserved recognition as artists, and that
the world needed to see their work, which represented an
unspoiled indigenous culture that had much to teach us. With
his usual persistence and determination, Juan succeeded in
finding the artists, in many cases becoming accepted as their

compadres and being welcomed into the Huichol communities in their remote ancestral lands in the Sierra Madre mountains of Mexico. This led to a decade's long involvement with
the Huichol, helping to promote the artists and their work,
and more significantly helping the Huichol defend their land
and communities from encroachment and exploitation. He
had lived with them in the Huichol mountains, gone on their
peyote pilgrimages, and somehow amidst all that managed
with his wife Yvonne to raise three beautiful daughters.
In the process Juan was to become a leading authority on
Huichol language, culture, and religion. By the late 1990s he
had moved back to the Bay Area from Guadalajara, his base
in Mexico, mostly for health reasons. For most of his adult
life he suffered from epilepsy and debilitating seizures which
were controlled by a regimen of very strong drugs, rendering
his accomplishments even more remarkable. When he called
me in 2001 the plan was to organize his extensive collection
of photographs and other materials into an online archive
which could be accessed by the Huichol and the general
public, and for this purpose he hoped to establish a nonprofit
which could raise funds and support this endeavor.

Juan photographing a yarn painting

My acquaintance with Juan led to me becoming his companion on several of his trips back to Mexico in the coming
years, partly because due to his epilepsy it was not advisable
for him to travel alone. Usually, we would stay at the home
of his eldest daughter in Bugambilias, an exclusive gated
community spread over the hills outside Guadalajara. Then
we would take a bus to Tepic where the largest population
of Huichol outside their traditional territory resided. The
impetus for these trips was Juan's desire to reconnect with
friends and associates and spend time in the country he
loved. Like my mother, he detested the culture and politics
of the United States (President Bush, he declared, was the
Antichrist).

It was in Mexico that Juan seemed to feel most at home,
and where his true persona could best emerge. To me Juan
was the most Christ-like figure I had ever known. His compas-
sion and selfless desire to serve humanity was coupled with
a deep sense of humility. Unlike some other outsiders who
would develop interest in the Huichol, Juan had absolutely
no presumption of becoming a shaman himself, of acquir-
ing notoriety or a coterie of followers, or of profiting off his
connections. And he was fearless, never one to avoid a confrontation. Walking down the streets of Tepic, if he spotted
a local wearing a t-shirt with an American flag, he wouldn't
hesitate to give them a piece of his mind. Once, after arriving
at his daughter's house and taking an evening stroll around
Bugambilias, a police car slowed down as it approached us.
One of the officers leaned out the window and asked where he
was going (people normally didn't walk in Bugambilias). "No
es asunto de usted!" (none of your business!) Juan snapped.
Miraculously, the officer just smiled and drove on. Similarly,
being asked for IDs by a policeman on a bus to Tepic, Juan
refused. Once again, the officer backed off. Perhaps they

sensed they were not dealing with an ordinary mortal.

On another occasion, I was certain we had met our end. Juan desired to connect with his compadre Yauxali to discuss a collection of stone carvings he had created that were in Juan's custody in California. For reasons unknown to me, Yauxali had been banished from the Huichol community of Santa Catarina and was living on a small ranch near Compostela, on the road from Tepic to Puerta Vallarta. As usual, Juan complained that I was driving too slowly. But soon enough he directed me to park next to what appeared to be an abandoned restaurant. From there we would have to hike to the ranch. Juan seemed not certain of the route, but nonetheless we set off up a dirt road in what he felt was the general direction. Soon, to my horror, we encountered a group of three locals who were armed to the teeth with rifles, machetes, and who knows what else. "Going hunting," they said. Juan asked if they knew where the Huichol ranch was, and they told us to just follow them. *How convenient,* I thought. Here we are out in the wilderness, far from the main road, where we could be murdered, robbed of our passports and money and never be heard from again. I tried to feign nonchalance. Juan, however, could not pass up the opportunity to provoke. "Why do you Mexicans call the Huichol 'Huicholitos'" (little Huichols) he asked. To him that was a term of derision commonly used by non-Huichol, and he wanted to know why. I don't recall the response. One of the three fell back and walked next to me.

"Your friend likes marijuana, no?" he asked.

I saw no point in denying it. "Si, senor," I replied. He just smiled.

After walking about half an hour, we came to a fork in the road. "Up there," they indicated. With a great sense of relief, we went right, and they went left.

"Were you worried?" I asked Juan.

"Yes, of course," he admitted. "I was praying powerfully the whole way to get us through." One might have assumed Juan was not religious, but in fact he considered himself, in addition to an existentialist, an ecumenical Christian and that faith seemed to give him needed strength when the situation required.

We soon arrived at Yauxali's ranch. A couple of young Huichol in their twenties came running down from the modest house carrying large knives to challenge us until they realized it was Juan. Yauxali himself was in the driveway sanding his truck in preparation for a new paint job. Unlike pictures I had seen of him in his younger days, when he was a dashing shaman in traditional garb, he had become a paunchy older man of unremarkable appearance. "Hola, compadre!" Juan exclaimed effusively, striding up the driveway to greet his friend. Yauxali shot him a brief glance, then continued with his work. They had not seen each other for several years but, Juan explained, as we went to sit with his wife and grown children, when they are in the middle of doing something the Huichol do not care to be interrupted.

Juan had been advised by Huichol elders that to cure his epilepsy it was necessary to make a pilgrimage to the kieri tree. The kieri—also known to the Huichol as the Tree of the Wind—is a member of the Solandra family which grows on rocky hillsides in upper elevations of the Huichol territory. Possessing powerful psychotropic properties, it has played a significant role in Huichol mythology and culture, almost equivalent to peyote, but not widely known to the outside world. Like other Huichol customs it was suppressed by the Spaniards and its worship went underground. Even today, there is allegedly a church in Tenzompa where the Huichol go to worship the kieri in the disguise of a Catholic saint. The Huichol make pilgrimages to the kieri seeking to enlist its power to fulfill their wishes to become better hunters, better musicians, to ward off witchcraft, or help them become shamans. But unlike peyote, kieri possesses a dark side which can inflict torment and even death on those who do not approach it with humility and sincerity. Juan told of several cases where outsiders, interested only in having a psychedelic trip, had been driven mad as the result of their encounter.

Unlike other psychedelics, kieri is not ingested; it is said that the pollen itself contains powerful entheogens and mere proximity to the tree produces profound psychotropic effects. According to myth, its pollen contains the divine essence from which the first Huichol shaman was born. And it was the power of the kieri that held the key to Juan's healing. There would be required a month of abstaining from salt and all sexual activities, followed by an arduous climb to the site of the kieri, the making of offerings, and a nightlong vigil by its side accompanied by a shaman.

A preparatory trip was made in which Juan handed over money to his compadre Guadalupe Gonzalez, an artist and shaman of some renown, to pay for the killing of a deer, the blood from which would provide the offering. Guadalupe was also to arrange for a shaman to accompany us on the pilgrimage, he himself being too old for the journey.

With great anticipation, mixed with some anxiety, I accompanied Juan on our return trip to Tepic for the actual pilgrimage. A friend of Juan drove us in his truck to the ranch of Guadalupe, located in the hills north of Tepic. The route required that we pass through a community of fundamentalist Christian Huicholes. I was told that relations between them and the traditional Huicholes were not exactly amicable, but we made it through safely, arriving around midday.

Guadalupe was seated in the yard outside the front door of his modest house. Juan introduced me, recounting how I was a lawyer who had helped them set up their organization, and how I had once been lawyer for Greenpeace.

"Tan bueno, tan bueno," Guadalupe kept repeating with a smile.

The ranch that day presented a remarkable scene. Next to his house was a large pavilion, much larger than the house itself, inside of which had been set up several tables manned by Huichol offering handicrafts for sale. Sprawled around the ranch was an assortment of gringos who had just returned from a trip to the desert to take peyote, led by a guide from California. Looking dazed and wasted, no doubt from a combination of the long trip and the effects of the peyote, they were not doing any shopping for souvenirs. Several of them would be leaving the following day for a trek to the kieri tree led by the same guide. Juan wanted no part of this group.

Had the deer whose blood was to be offered to the kieri been killed as arranged in our prior visit? No, it had not, Guadalupe admitted. I can't say I was displeased by this news. I could never understand why the Huichol ancestors found happiness in the needless killing of an innocent animal.

Had Guadalupe found a suitable shaman to accompany us on the pilgrimage? No, he had not.

"You can be the shaman," Guadalupe suggested of Juan.

"Me? Be my own shaman? No, no, no," Juan scoffed. "I am not a shaman!"

Was Guadalupe certain, was there no one who could take them? There was no one.

"In that case," Juan said without hesitating, "We are not going."

Juan seemed unperturbed by this setback, but I felt

deflated. Unlike Juan, I had no compelling reason to visit the kieri, but had nonetheless looked forward to the experience. I wandered around the ranch aimlessly until Juan came up to me and asked, "Did Guadalupe give you any peyote?" No, he had not.

"Well, he told me he did. But here, you can have some of mine."

We ate our peyote and climbed into the truck for the drive back to Tepic. Sitting in a truck driving down from the hills over a bumpy road was probably not the optimal setting for a peyote experience. But the dose was a mild one and it felt soft and gentle, suffusing every cell of my body with a warm and comforting glow, making me feel connected to the earth and all of creation.

Back in Tepic, we went for dinner to a seafood restaurant which served giant seafood cocktails. Juan did not eat his.

"Are you not going to have this?" his friend asked.

"No," Juan replied. His friend, obviously a man of big appetites, downed it in a few swift gulps.

Since we had a few days to kill before our flight home, it was decided to take a road trip to Michoacan with Juan's daughter, her husband, and their daughter Sofia. I knew of Michoacan only from my drug dealing days when it was a source of high-quality marijuana. For me the trip was a magical experience, spending time with the playful and innocent six-year-old Sofia. It made me wonder if, now almost sixty, I would ever experience the joy of having a child. None of my four marriages had produced any offspring.

After a long drive we spent the night in Urapan, then drove to Lake Pátzcuaro where we took a boat to the island of Janitzio dominated by its huge statue of José María Morelos. Then we went for a horseback ride up the slopes of Paricutin Volcano, one of the many volcanic cones that dot the landscape of Michoacan, before driving back to Guadalajara. I was sad to say goodbye to Sofia, and to know that the trip to the kieri would likely never take place.

Juan and Sofia on Lake Pátzcuaro, Mexico

J uan and I would return to Mexico one more time. He had been invited to attend the Festival of the First Fruits, held every October to celebrate the corn harvest. It took place in the ceremonial center of the Santa Catarina community in the Huichol mountains. Of the several communities that shared the Huichol territory, Santa Catarina was the one with which Juan was closely associated, and it was the most conservative of them all, seldom allowing outsiders and not permitting cameras or recording devices in their territory. The ceremonial center, known as Las Latas, could only be reached on foot. It consisted of a series of wood structures, including a main temple, arranged in a circle around a central patio. Juan was also going to use this visit to present his plan to install a computer in the school in Santa Catarina so they could have access to the online archive he was creating.

We were driven from Guadalajara by Juan's friend Patricia Diaz. Patricia was the daughter of a successful media mogul whose career had started as a busboy at the Biltmore Hotel in Los Angeles, eventually accumulating a collection of Mexican radio and television stations. He built a walled compound consisting of several houses for his family in Guadalajara, but he also had an interest in the Huichol, allowing use of one of his radio stations to pass messages between Huichol in the mountains and Guadalajara. Patricia became a fierce

advocate for the Huichol and led a campaign to eliminate
the use of toxic pesticides in the tobacco fields worked by
Huichol laborers.

The first night was spent in the picturesque town of
Zacatecas, built on both sides of a narrow canyon. There we
visited the home of John and Colette Lilly. John, a filmmaker
and son of the famed counterculture scientist and thinker
of the same name, and Colette shared a lifelong interest in
the Huichol. Zacatecas was also home to a beautiful museum
which featured an impressive exhibit of Huichol art.

The following day we continued the drive up into the
Huichol territory to the tiny community of Nueva Colonia.
Patricia left us at the house of one of Juan's compadres,
Andres, where we would spend the night sleeping on the
floor of his kitchen. Patricia stayed with another group which
was to head to Las Latas on their own. Juan tried to convince
Andres to come to the festival and participate in the discussion of his plans for the archive, but Andres refused. I learned
he had some reason to be annoyed with Juan, as several years
earlier Juan had promised to watch over his daughter after
she had left the mountains to live in Puerto Vallarta, but he
had not followed through.

Juan and I were to hike on our own to Las Latas, situated
in a broad valley reached by a trail down a steep hillside. It
was decided we needed a donkey to carry our baggage, Juan
being in no condition to carry his own. A neighbor of Andres
happened to have one, so we marched off to their house to
see if we borrow it from its owner, Juan Garcia, a farmer with
three children. He was not at home, but his wife was in a good
mood and agreed to the loan.

Donkey in tow we headed back for a traditional breakfast
of blue corn tortillas and bean soup with a little bowl of salsa
on the side served to us by Andres's wife. One is supposed to

form pieces of the tortillas into the shape of little spoons with which to eat the soup, but it seemed that both Juan and I had difficulty mastering this simple technique.

When it was time to leave Juan took the donkey's rope and led it out across a meadow with me in the rear. Juan had to struggle to get the donkey moving, so out of frustration he handed the rope to me and the donkey followed along reluctantly, stopping to snack on mouthfuls of grasses and tasty plants whenever he could.

Eventually we came to a fork in the path. Juan was unsure of the way and chose a path that led us down the side of a steep and treacherous heavily wooded hill. At the bottom was a clearing with a small house. No one seemed to be at home. From there we took a trail that went off to the right and followed it for about half an hour before giving up and returning to the house. This time he decided we should go straight, following a trail which went down into a canyon. This was clearly a bad choice and the donkey rebelled by sitting down in the path, carefully balancing his load so it did not tip over. After a few exhortations he got back up and we made a right turn, struggling up a hill until we encountered a Huichol woman astride a donkey who directed us in a different direction. We followed this new path until it eventually returned us to the clearing with the house. We had wasted two hours making this torturous loop. Now Juan decided to take the only remaining option, the trail to the left. It led through some swampy meadows and eventually to the edge of a steep canyon. We stupidly considered going down into the canyon, but it was getting dark and we came to our senses and turned back. We arrived at a stone wall, found an opening in it, and walked across a wide meadow to another stone wall with another opening. It was not wide enough for us to pass through so I started removing some of the stones. But by this time Juan could barely stand up from exhaustion and it was getting darker by the minute, so we decided to stop and spend the night outdoors and try to find our way in the morning.

Pondering our situation, my main concern was that it would be easy to unpack the donkey, but I had no confidence in our ability to load him up again in the morning. Suddenly the donkey set off on his own up a path. I had a feeling he was onto something, so I followed along behind him with Juan in the rear. We rounded the crest of a small hill where the trail merged with a larger one. Up ahead on the right I could see a strange apparition, what looked like a glowing ember suspended eerily in the now dark night air. Getting closer we could see that it was a Huichol standing motionless holding a burning branch about a hundred feet off the path. What he was doing there at that time was a mystery. Juan went up to him and began a conversation with the obvious admission that he was lost. To my surprise, the Huichol recognized Juan, although Juan did not recognize him. He had stayed at Juan's house several years before in Guadalajara. Many Huichol made visits outside the mountains when they became sick or for other reasons and Juan offered his house as a refuge during these visits, often to the dismay of his daughter whose room was often appropriated for their use. As the Huichol had always extended hospitality to him in the mountains, he could hardly fail to return the favor when they visited Guadalajara, he explained.

The Huichol, a man named Antonio, agreed to let us stay with him for the night, so he took charge of the donkey and led us there. It was no surprise to me that he lived in the very same house that we had already passed three times before. I mentioned this to Juan, but he became quite angry and insisted we had never passed by there before. "All the houses up here look the same!" he barked. Of course, that was the only house we had seen the whole time.

The next morning Antonio loaded up the donkey and said he would lead us to the ceremonial center, but after a short while he simply pointed the way and turned back to go home. I was worried we would get lost again, but fortunately we managed to find our way. It was a two hour hike to the other side of a range of hills from where we had wandered aimlessly for eight hours the day before.

Upon arrival at the ceremonial site Juan led us to a compound where the eldest of the Huichol elders lived. He also was a compadre of Juan and was supposedly very ill, but he wasn't there. Instead his son welcomed us and showed us to a small hut where we stayed, sharing the space with a family of chickens. I tied the donkey to a tree inside the compound, giving him access to a small patch of corn growing nearby which he enjoyed until the son took him outside the compound and tied him up on a small knoll where he would spend the next two days alone. Feeling sorry for him, I would occasionally stop by and pat him on the neck, realizing it was probably a sign of affection which meant nothing to him.

The ceremonial center was like a small village arranged around a central clearing. It is used only for ceremonies that take place at certain times of the year. At one corner of the clearing is a large round temple building with a tall, thatched roof. Smaller temples and "god houses" built by individual Huichol surround the circle, along with other small buildings used as communal accommodations by Huichol from outside the immediate area and for food preparation. The center is nestled against a high cliff in a beautiful, lush valley surrounded by mountains with long sweeping ridges punctuated by arrow shaped peaks. The land is blanketed with oak and pine forests interspersed with meadows covered with wildflowers of many colors and, in the immediate area of the center, corn fields tended by those who live in the area. There is no electricity and, at least at the time of our visit, no access by road.

The Festival of the First Fruits takes place in October at the time of the corn harvest and must be completed before anyone can partake of the fruits of that harvest. It is a family event and the children participate in all aspects. There is drumming, chanting, music and dancing, all of which have a quality of sweetness and gentleness which pleasantly surprised me. The celebration begins around noon on the first day with drumming and chanting. The children are given rattles and play along for hours. This is part of their training so they can learn discipline and feel part of the community. At sunset there is a short break when food is served, including tortillas of all different kinds, guava fruits, and bowls of beef broth. Then the ceremony moves inside the temple for more chanting, drumming, music and dancing, continuing all night until noon the following day, when each person comes to an altar to receive a blessing and a symbolic ration of corn from the new harvest.

Besides Juan, Patricia and myself there were three other outsiders who were there working on a project to increase the stock of deer in the mountains. An additional mysterious presence was a quiet young woman from Bosnia. After dinner was served Juan sat down next to her and asked where she was from. "Bosnia," she answered. Juan asked her opinion of Tito, the former strongman leader of Yugoslavia, of which Bosnia had been a part, who had been a friend of Juan's grandfather. The woman admitted to having a certain respect for him. Asked why she was there, she explained that the year before she had taken peyote and had not felt well since.

"Do you know about brujos?" she asked. Juan thought for a minute before answering.

"Yes, there were once men who were considered witches, but they were not really witches. They were accused of that by the Catholic church, and it was done only to persecute them." That was not what she hoped to hear. Someone had advised her to find a mixed blood medicine man, a brujo, who could cure her and that was why she was here. Juan disagreed with this advice.

"The mestizos do not know as much as the Huichol," he said. "Before taking peyote, the Huichol say that you must perform a fast, and you must also confess your sexual sins, not in private like the Catholics do, but in public for everyone to hear. That is probably what is causing your physical problems, that you have not confessed your sexual sins." I wondered what her reaction to this advice was, before Juan concluded, "But you should not take peyote tonight because you have eaten." The woman thanked him sincerely and that was the last we saw of her.

After the ceremonies we decided to leave the site together with Patricia and the other visitors. The donkey was loaded up with our packs and we headed up the switchback trail that led up the mountain to Nueva Colonia. Juan had been given some peyote and most of the group consumed some on the way up. Juan explained that the Huichol used it to help them walk long distances, but this ascent only took about an hour, in contrast to our ordeal on the way down. At the top was parked the truck in which Patricia had come and everyone began to pile in.

"Get in," Patricia urged, "we can pull the donkey from inside the truck," but I refused.

"No, I have too much respect for this donkey to allow him to be dragged along behind a truck!" I exclaimed. "I will walk behind the truck with the donkey."

I didn't realize that we were still an hour and a half from our destination, but no one seemed in a hurry. It was just before sunset and the dirt road took us along a beautiful mountain-top plateau with its lush meadows and forests. Eventually Patricia got out and walked with us. A Huichol woman came towards us out of a field carrying only a small basket with a few ears of corn. She was wearing a colorful traditional dress and we were in awe of her beauty.

"Do you know where we can find the ranch of Juan Garcia?" Patricia asked. We were very near by now. The Huichol waved across the field in the correct general direction, then admired the scarf that Patricia was wearing. Patricia took it off and gave it to the woman, who thanked her and walked off down the road.

Although I had led the donkey the entire way, Juan got out of the truck and insisted that it would be better if he delivered it back to its owner. Juan Garcia was not at home and we were greeted instead by his eldest daughter. She seemed excited to see us and received us warmly. Juan asked her what the price was for the four days of donkey rental. She shrugged, then suggested fifty pesos. Juan thought we should give them a bit more, and I proposed one hundred. Juan balked, thinking it a bit much, but I lied, saying I only had one-hundred-peso bills.

"Does the donkey have a name?" Patricia asked. Again, a shrug. It was not customary to give donkeys a name. "Well then, we shall name him Juan!" Patricia exclaimed.

"Yes, Juan Negrin!" I added. The daughter grinned. That was fine with her. The donkey stood silently feigning disregard, as we walked off giddily into the fading evening light.

My friend Juan continued his work on behalf of the Huichol until his death in 2015 from the complications of epilepsy. The last year of his life was spent in the hospital, a horrible end to a remarkable life.

I reconnected with Bob Taunt, my Greenpeace friend, after he and his wife Suzanne moved to Carmel from Montana in 2005 and built their dream house, which I visited many times. After Greenpeace, Bob became active with the Nature Conservancy and explored the South Pacific putting together a collection of aboriginal art. He died in 2014 after a long battle with lymphoma.

Outliving my mother by over twenty years, my father died of a heart attack in 2005, just short of his ninety-first birthday. He retired from UC Berkeley in 1984 and never remarried, but at the time of his death he had two lovers.

After my fourth wife and I divorced in 1994, I also would never marry again. There would be other romances and numerous women, and I would discover a new infatuation with the city of Paris, travelling there often—usually by myself—and exploring all the wonderful regions of France. Once, driving back to Paris through the Ile de France, smoking a cigarette, listening to Radio FIP, I almost imagined myself becoming a Frenchman, but of course that was as close as I was to get.

By some miracle the software business I started in 1985

continues to thrive to the present day. But the greatest miracle of all is that in 2012 I met a wonderful woman who happened to have a two-year-old daughter named Apple. Apple and I bonded, fulfilling the vision I had with Sofia in Mexico, and I became her virtual grandpa, spending endless hours playing with dolls, reading to her, hanging out at the Claremont Hotel pool. To help her grow into the happy, thriving teenager she is today has been the greatest joy of my life. Although I still see her often, we no longer play with dolls, and she no longer wants me to read to her—but her cousin has a beautiful husky dog with whom I spend endless hours walking the streets of San Francisco and roaming the beaches of the Presidio. Dave—the name is just a coincidence—is a very happy dog.

With Dave at Fort Point, San Francisco, 2023

www.ingramcontent.com/pod-product-compliance
Lightning Source LLC
Chambersburg PA
CBHW022006090426
42741CB00007B/915